Study Smarter,
Not Harder

Study Smarter, Not Harder

Kevin Paul, M.A.

Self-Counsel Press
(a division of)
International Self-Counsel Press Ltd.
U.S.A. Canada

Printed in Canada

First edition: 1996; Reprinted: 1997; 1999; 2002 (2); 2003

Canadian Cataloguing in Publication Data

Paul, Kevin, 1958-
    Study smarter, not harder

    (Self-counsel series)
    Includes index
    ISBN 1-55180-059-4
    Study skills — Handbooks, manuals, etc. I. Title. II. Series.
LB1049.P38 1996   371.3'028'12   C96-910664-5

Cartoons by Carole Klemm © 1996

Self-Counsel Press
(a division of)
International Self-Counsel Press Ltd.

1704 N. State Street   1481 Charlotte Road
Bellingham, WA   98225   North Vancouver, BC   V7J 1H1
          U.S.A.   Canada

Contents

Exercises

Figures

Samples

To my parents, Doreen and Clive Paul. I love to learn.
That wonderful gift is from them and I carry it
with me always.

And to students of all ages who want to be
the best learners they can possibly be — and to the
parents who wish this gift for their children.

Acknowledgments

This book contains many of my own ideas and interpretations of the ideas of others. However, I would not be in a position to have ideas and interpretations had it not been for the opportunities I was given at the beginning of my career and the work of inspirational researchers and writers in the field of learning and study skills.

I want to thank Dr. Horace Beach for the leap of faith he took when he hired me as an inexperienced study skills instructor. I am deeply indebted and grateful to Dr. Joe Parsons and Shirley Henderson for being my mentors and colleagues in the Learning Skills department of Counselling Services at the University of Victoria.

There are several superb books that, over the years, have been the foundation of my own view of study skills. The best of these come from the work of Walter Pauk, Howard Gardner, Colin Rose, and Tony Buzan. I recommend that you read them as well as this book.

Karin Paul provided insight from her vantage point as a high school teacher and university instructor. I also thank her for being patient with me while this book came together.

Speaking of patience . . .

Ruth Wilson deserves some kind of medal for her understanding and forbearance as the manuscript came to her in several pieces. Her professionalism, creativity, and talent, and that of her editorial department, have taken this book to a much higher level than I could ever do on my own.

Notwithstanding the notable vigilance of the editors (I am constantly amazed at the level of detailed work that goes on in the editing process), any errors you might find should be attributed to me alone.

Part I

Introduction

1.

The knowledge explosion

Did you know that the **rate** of new information is **doubling** every six months?   Did you know that **most** of what you learn today will be **obsolete** in two years?

Are you **worried** about how to keep up? Are you bewildered by the information explosion at **school?** at **work?** at **home?** Does it have you feeling worried?

Stressed?

Overwhelmed?

Space is big. Really big. You just won't believe how vastly hugely mindbogglingly big it is. I mean you may think it's a long way down the road to the chemist, but that's just peanuts to space.

Douglas Adams

TAKE HEART! The solution to your problems and anxiety is closer than you might believe. The answer is already between your ears.

You already have the engine you need — your brain — to adapt and thrive in a world where you have to keep learning new things. All you need are the tools to get that engine running at a higher level of efficiency than it is now.

How much room for improvement do you have? Just think of it this way. Your mind power and learning potential are like space. What you actually use is peanuts compared to your capacity. The unused potential is like the vastness of unexplored space.

No matter what your present level of learning ability and achievement may be, YOU CAN DO BETTER!

- If you're failing, you can pass.
- If you're passing, you can get Bs.
- If you're getting Bs, you can get As.
- If you're getting As, you can do even better!

What does it take to start down the road to achieving the kind of learning mastery that your potential promises? It takes three things:

(a) Desire to be a better learner. Picking up a book like this is a start. It shows that you want to expand your horizons.

(b) Belief in yourself. High self-esteem is a vital ingredient for success in any activity, and this is especially true of studying and learning. Chapters 2 and 3 will give you some of the basic foundation for looking at your learning ability in a whole new way. This foundation is meant to show that your potential to earn As in anything is not a myth. Chapters 4, 5, and 6 will show you how to build on that belief in yourself and to activate it in each study session.

(c) A bottomless toolbox. Desire and self-esteem are good things, but they are useless without some ways to build on that foundation and make practical use of it. A house is only as strong as its foundation, but you can't live in a foundation. You have to build on it. The chapters in Part III show you how to develop study tools that will build on your foundation.

Now it's up to you to take the next step: a step away from the anxiety about your school work and the eruption of information in the world and a step toward developing the kind of mind that can handle all this with ease and fun for the rest of your life.

Remember Thomas Edison's words if the going gets a little tough along the way:

"Many of life's failures are those people who did not realize how close they were to success when they gave up."

2.

You can learn anything

Congratulations on taking the first step along the path of life-long mastery.

Mastery of what? You can master anything you want to learn. Whether it's your high school diploma, college career program, university degree courses, sales training seminar, or professional licensing exam, there is no limit. You can learn anything you want — if you unlock the genius inside you. The possibilities and potential are extraordinarily exciting.

u. You are a genius

Yes, you read that correctly. It does say GENIUS!

This book is about how to bring out the genius inside you. That's right! You have the potential to learn and achieve learning results at the true genius level.

This is not an exaggeration. There are ways of studying and learning that are painful, arduous, and, ultimately, fruitless, and you are left worse off than before. You probably have some personal experience of this kind of "education."

Conversely, there are ways of learning and patterns of study that not only help make you more knowledgeable, but also increase your inherent intelligence. Does that sound impossible? Isn't intelligence set in stone when you're born and there is nothing you can do to change it?

Think about it. Research shows that spending countless hours as a couch potato in front of the TV will actually reduce your I.Q. And if it can change in a negative direction, then it can certainly be coached into the positive.

Believe it or not, you are already an incredibly efficient learner. Acquiring a language and walking are two of the most complex activities in which humans engage. It is not yet possible to get enough computing power to synthesize these basic human achievements. It takes a very sophisticated learning capability to achieve language and walking. Research shows that even driving a car takes more brain power than piloting the lunar excursion module that landed on the moon.

Just to give yourself a review of what a good learner you already are, do the following exercise. Write down all the things in your life that you have learned that have nothing to do with formal classroom schooling. Here is a list to start with — some or all may apply to you:

- Walk and run
- Talk — in at least one language
- Ride a bike
- Drive a car
- Swim
- Give directions
- Plant a garden
- Paint your house

- Iron clothes
- Babysit
- Build model airplanes
- Bake bread

Make your own list. It will show you just how proficient you have become as a basic learner without really trying. Imagine what you could accomplish if you worked at it with the right coaching.

Chapter 3 will give you a simple overview of how your brain and "intelligences" work. You will see just how natural it can be to get your mind working at genius levels. Human beings normally use only 2% to 10% (depending on which expert you read) of the brain's capacity for high-level thought. Imagine what you would be capable of if you knew how to access the rest of that potential. Even if you learn how to activate only a small portion of that untapped reservoir, you can achieve things you only dreamed of before.

That quality we think of as "genius" is not beyond your current capabilities. In fact, genius level is only utilizing a marginally higher percentage of the brain's enormous potential. Genius seems exclusive and unattainable only because so few people actually perform at that level. But it is there for you with the proper kind of training. It's there for you if you're willing to work for it.

There is no magic involved: no drugs, divine intervention, or mind-altering tricks. There is nothing extraordinarily difficult involved. In fact, when you begin to follow the strategies and "mind workout" exercises provided in this book, you will be amazed at how much common sense is involved. Once you know the keys to accessing the brain's power, the skills needed to develop that power seem obvious.

However, this is not a quick fix to study and learning problems. You have to commit yourself to a persistent, consistent practice of the kinds of skills that can transform you into a superlearner. But if you spend your time wisely, if you study smarter and never give up, the results will amaze you. There will be noticeable improvements almost immediately, but the permanent leaps forward in performance won't come until after several months of work. If you stick with it, your results and achievements will shout to everyone that you are a genius.

What counts is not the number of hours you put in but how much you put into those hours.

Anonymous

b. Who can do this?

The only limitation to this approach is that it works best for young adults (senior high school) and older. Younger children generally need more guidance, although some of the exercises can apply. In fact, it's never too early for parents and teachers to encourage young children to enjoy learning using all the different kinds of "intelligences," but the specific study skills in this book are not appropriate for them.

There is no upper age limit to using this approach. Any age. Any time in life. No matter where and when you're starting from, you can increase your intelligence and learning ability. It's a misconception that you lose the ability to learn new things or learn them fast as you get older. The truth is that your intelligence is like a muscle: if you don't use it, you lose it. Conversely, if you exercise it, it does get stronger. Chapter 3 covers some of the physiology of the brain that makes this possible.

This approach will work on any learning task. You will achieve unparalleled success in any setting: formal schooling, formal training and exams, personal learning projects, and informal learning settings. You will see positive results regardless of any previous bad experiences with formal learning in schools. Your past does not have to equal your future. In fact, the worse you did in school, the more quickly you see the difference now.

c. How is this possible?

Your brain is like a supercomputer that has been installed and activated, but didn't come with an instruction manual. Consider this your introductory course in how to use your supercomputer.

The belief in your genius potential is based on the reality of the brain's biology and physiology and what the last 30 years of scientific research tell us about intelligence. Chapter 3 gives you some background on how it all works, and then chapters 4, 5, and 6 show you how to use it to help you work on improving three of the basic foundations of superlearning: preparation, memory, and concentration.

Why does this approach work? Because it is natural. It recognizes the way you naturally learn and helps you to REdiscover how to use it.

d. Why it is important to unlock your genius

Among the few things more expensive than an education these days is the lack of it.

Anonymous

Being a successful learner is no longer a matter of choice or mere preference. It is a necessity in order to survive and thrive in the "information age." The future belongs to learners. As we are constantly told by the various media, we live in a time of rapid change. And the pace of that change is faster than at any other time in human history. Every year, 20% to 30% of what we learned and understood about our world is obsolete.

Until recently — the late 19th and 20th centuries — it has been muscle power that has dominated individual success. Despite humankind's growing intellectual capabilities, most individual successes as a hunter/gatherer in the Stone Age, farmer in the Agricultural Age, or factory worker in the Industrial Age depended on physical capacity for hard manual work.

Today and in the future, it is mind power that will dominate. Wealth and jobs are no longer in the land or physical commodities. Knowledge is wealth. Knowledge is where the careers and security are.

When you combine the astonishing rate of knowledge obsolescence with the fact that knowledge is now the most valuable commercial commodity on earth, you begin to understand the value of learning how to learn. You also begin to see school and university subjects in a whole new light.

It isn't the content that matters necessarily, because that will likely be meaningless in a few years — especially in the sciences and technology. Rather, it is the training you are receiving in learning how to learn that is the primary value. Each subject makes a contribution to training and exercises a different "intelligence."

As you will read in chapter 3, you actually have several "intelligences," not just one. Learning math, history, chemistry, music, and art all help train a different intelligence. You need to develop all your intelligences if you are going to take full advantage of your brain's almost unlimited capacity to learn.

You can develop this on your own if you're not in school at the moment. But, if you are in school, you have the perfect variable training ground to use the techniques and concepts in this book. Just as an athlete uses different approaches to improve various areas of his or her physical capabilities — running to develop aerobic capacity, weight training to increase muscle strength, stretching to enhance flexibility — the super-learner must become comfortable with developing many intelligences, not just the dominant one or two with which he or she feels comfortable.

Teaching yourself how to learn is the most valuable skill you can learn today. It's no longer enough to have the attitude that your learning days are over at high school graduation or when you have your bachelor's degree. To be successful in a world where knowledge is the key, you must be skilled and fluent in acquiring knowledge and making it part of you. This will be a continual process. Learn to learn, and love it, or you will fall behind and struggle all your life.

There are costs and risks to any program of action, but they are far less than the long range risks and costs of comfortable inaction.

John F. Kennedy

I believe that the biggest mistake educational planners are making today is to bleat on about the necessity of making our schools, colleges, and universities more relevant by focusing on skills training. This is a foolish waste of time. Our fast-paced, technological society is changing so quickly that any specific skills taught and knowledge imparted will be 50% useless by the time the graduate is finished the program. It will be almost 100% useless by the time he or she has been in the workforce for two years. In an age when knowledge is the chief source of wealth, the only truly timeless skill is that which gives you the ability to keep learning for the rest of your life. If your formal schooling doesn't give you that, then you have to get it for yourself. Reading and using this book is your first step.

But if outside circumstances force you to become a lifelong learner, it is the sheer joy of the achievement that will keep you on that path. Learning is natural and fun — just ask any infant (if you can master the intricacies of the child's language). The key to your future is entirely in your control and the possibilities it opens up are truly exciting.

e. Where to start

This book first gives you a short overview of the theory and foundation skills (Part II) and then provides a series of practical exercises and strategies that will become the starting point of your own lifelong love affair with learning (Part III). The practical hints and strategies in Part III can be put to use immediately if you have an urgent need to improve a certain area.

Some are geared toward a "get fit" attitude about getting your brain in shape and learning anything you want to in life. There are also specific strategies and exercises that focus on the particular kind of learning in the formal education settings of school, university, or professional courses for, for example, insurance and real estate licenses.

You should begin by reading chapters 3 and 4 together. Then you should take the basic principles of chapter 4, prepare yourself properly, and study chapter 3 again. The ideas in these two chapters form the thread that runs through the rest of the book and ties all the exercises and suggestions together. Even the smallest study hint is designed in keeping with the way the brain works and how your various "intelligences" need to be stimulated.

f. What to expect

Expect to fail . . . at first. You won't fail because you are dumb or because it's too hard to do this stuff, but rather because of humankind's normal resistance to change. The condition called *homeostasis* resists change in any organism, even if that change is ultimately beneficial. It takes time to get your system accustomed to doing things differently. Therefore, startling positive results won't be immediate; they will be slow and incremental. But they are real. In fact, if you truly make a commitment to lifelong learning as an unending part of your life, the results will come faster than you might expect — just not quite as fast as you would like.

Failing and making mistakes are the only way to make true progress in something new. It has been said that the only way to be staggeringly successful is to double your rate of failure. That is not as silly as it may seem. If you don't make mistakes, you aren't pushing yourself into new realms of possibility. Failure is normal at the beginning of something new or unfamiliar. Failure also fades away as you make an effort; do not stop until successes far outnumber mistakes.

Therefore, you must also expect to put in a lot of effort. The work that's needed to be done is easy and relatively simple, but it's also new and, therefore, likely to be uncomfortable at first. It takes effort to overcome that discomfort and explore new things. Find the energy for that effort and you will be richly rewarded!

Expect to be persistent. If you fail a lot, put in a lot of effort, and still do not see the promised results, DO NOT GIVE UP. Change strategies, review what you are doing, try something new. But if you stick to the principles in this book, you *will* succeed.

Most important, expect to see a vast array of positive results:

- Develop a toolbox of learning techniques that can bring you success on any learning task.

- Quadruple your study efficiency.

- Expand your memory capacity up to 100 times and beyond.

- Double and even triple your reading speed and comprehension.

His [the man of genius] errors are volitional and are the portals of discovery.

James Joyce

Genius is 1% inspiration and 99% perspiration.

Thomas Edison

A genius! For thirty-seven years I've practiced fourteen hours a day, and now they call me a genius!

Pablo Sarasate
(Spanish violinist and composer)

- Develop unstoppable motivation to achieve your learning goals.
- Learn how to use music and ancient relaxation techniques to supercharge your studying.
- Discover how to make each learning task fit your personal learning style for amazing results.

Expect to find some tips and hints that will work immediately. You will experience the best results if you take time to load up your "toolbox" with many skills and new viewpoints on learning. However, if your problem right now is getting through one particularly difficult textbook, the chapter on reading will work very well just by itself.

Finally, throughout the book, ideas and concepts are repeated in several different places. This is done on purpose. As you will read in later chapters, repetition is the mother of skill — it is how things get into your long-term memory.

g. Personal responsibility

In the past, education has always been something that has been done *to* you. You have been trained to sit passively and accept the teaching that is given to you by the teacher, trainer, or professor. If education didn't "happen" to you, it was easy to blame the ineffectiveness of the teacher.

In the long run you hit only what you aim at. Therefore, though you should fail immediately, you had better aim at something high.

Henry David Thoreau

Now you must change that attitude. You have to take personal responsibility for your own learning. Anyone who is at the senior high school age or older can understand the concepts of supercharged learning. Everyone at that age also has some kind of learning project they can use to train themselves in these methods and attitudes. If you don't have a learning project, you better get one — there is always something you could be studying to improve your credentials, grades, skills, and abilities.

Push yourself beyond your comfort zone. You don't need to go overboard, but you won't progress to exceptional levels unless you push yourself into areas you've never been before — such as singing your algebra lessons to yourself as a means of remembering formulas for the exam. (No one has to be around to hear you!)

Part II

The fundamentals

3.

Your astonishing brain and your amazing intelligences

> Your brain can keep learning from birth till the end of life.
>
> Dr. Marian Diamond

a. This chapter can change your life

Understanding the basics of your brain and your "intelligences" can literally change your life. It will change —

- your attitude to learning,
- your learning results,
- your creative output,
- your problem-solving ability, and
- your SUCCESS in any aspect of life that involves learning, which means any aspect of life!

This is not secret information. It is relatively recent, but it is based on the published work of eminent scientists and researchers (some won the Nobel Prize for their work) over the past 25 years. Many well-known practitioners and teachers have taken this research and made it available to the public through books, seminars, workshops, and tapes. Still, very few people are aware of this life-changing information. It is not a part of the official school or college curriculum. You need to make the effort to get it for yourself. Reading this book is a good first step.

This book takes the common elements of this revolution in learning and applies them to some elementary skills necessary for success in the formal school setting, as well as in the informal and formal learning situations of work training.

This chapter is a simple summary of some very complex research. It is presented here to give you a glimpse of the depths of the untapped potential in your brain and to help you understand the reason for the exercises, strategies, and tips being the way they are. There is a reason!

b. The numbers that will change your life

The information you need to understand the basics of your brain and your intelligences is organized around numbers. These numbers give you the insight to develop a clear vision of your own incredible potential. Did you know you have —

- trillions upon trillions of brain cells,
- one hundred billion neurons in your "thinking brain,"
- twenty thousand possible connections between neurons,
- seven "intelligences,"
- four wave lengths of brain wave patterns,
- three brains in one (the *triune* brain),
- three basic learning modalities,
- two sides to the higher brain, and
- one brain — everybody has one!?

c. There's more than one computer in there

The human brain has been described as the most powerful computer ever conceived. This is accurate as far as it goes. The brain is, in fact, an astonishingly powerful electro-biochemical supercomputer. But it is much more than that. The density of brain matter and the elegantly effective communication system between its various parts at the structural and microscopic level have pushed our thought processes beyond the merely mechanical. We are more than just vast computers with the storage capacity and numerous linear functions that implies. Our brain's biology has caused us to cross the threshold into a realm of complexity, creativity, and self-awareness that computer scientists can only dream of.

It is an understanding of the biology of the brain, along with the discoveries of scientists in the last 25 years, that leads experts to conclude that we are using only 2% to 10% of our potential capacity for higher thought. Understanding the implications of this research for our learning and studying is the beginning of getting access to the rest of that brain power.

1. Three brains in one

A cross section of a human brain clearly shows that there are actually three different brains in there. Dr. Paul McLean did the ground-breaking research in this area, and he noted very different activity in the three parts of what he termed the triune brain: the reptilian brain, the limbic brain, and the cortical brain. Each appears to have developed at different stages in human evolution.

TRIUNE BRAIN

(a) Reptilian brain

The most primitive part of the human brain was given the name "reptilian" because it governs the lowest levels of thought that result in the instinctive behavior we associate with reptiles. In addition to monitoring and regulating such basic autonomic bodily functions as breathing, heart rate, and hunger, the reptilian brain is also the home of our sense of territory and the "fight or flight" response to danger. Those instincts that are most closely connected with our safety and survival have their home in this most primitive part of our brain.

LOWER BRAIN

One element of the functioning of this part of the brain is particularly relevant to studying. When the reptilian brain is dominating our behavior (when we are being physically attacked and we are responding instinctively, for example), we have little access to our higher brain functions. They are blocked. In fact, any level of negative stress will have this effect, in varying degrees. This means that an optimum studying state of mind includes as little stress as possible.

(b) Limbic brain

The limbic, or middle, brain deals with more complex brain functions than its lower-level counterpart. It evolved after the reptilian brain and it is physically added on top.

MIDDLE BRAIN

This middle brain is also often referred to as the "mammalian" brain because it functions much the same as the brain in most other mammals. It is the primary home for emotions, regulation of the immune and hormonal systems, and sexuality.

Research also seems to indicate that the limbic brain is the primary site of long-term memory storage. This proximity to the home of our strongest emotional centers has obvious implications for memory and learning. As you will read in chapter 5, one of the major keys to memory is association and the strongest associations are those that have emotion in them. It makes sense if you think about it in terms of the things that are the most powerful memories in your life. What about your first love? Or the birth of a child? Or the death of a loved one? Or the best Christmas gift you ever received?

You can probably recall much more detail about such emotionally rich events that occurred years ago than you do about more mundane things that happened last week. Emotion is a key to strong memories.

(c) Cortical brain

HIGHER BRAIN

The activity that we think of as "higher" brain functions is physically located in the highest and outermost layer of the brain: the cortex. This is our thinking brain. It contains the higher "intelligences" such as our ability to reason, set goals and make plans, develop language, and conceive abstractly.

This layer of brain matter is only one-quarter of an inch thick, but its folds and convolutions (which make it look wrinkled) hide its enormous area. It is what makes sense of all the input we receive and organizes the various ways in which we know the world and ourselves.

(d) Three brains working as one

The three brains don't function in isolation from each other. They are connected by specialized cells and structures that serve as a communication link between them. When in the state of "relaxed alertness" that is best for effective studying, that communication link is open and very efficient. At times of great stress and physical or emotional danger, the connection to the higher brain functions is virtually shut down and we are controlled by our reptilian and limbic brains.

2. Getting your brain in shape for maximum learning

Your brain has many trillions of cells. In your higher brain — or cortex — you have over 100 billion active cells called neurons. Each individual neuron is more powerful than most computers on the planet. It has many millions of pumps and regulators dealing just with cell nutrition and sodium levels, never mind all the other functions of a neuron. It's amazing.

NEURONS

It is not, however, the number of these wonderful little supercomputers that determines intelligence. Each neuron has the potential to make 20,000 different connections with other neurons. It does so with structures called "dendrites" and "axons" which branch out of the main cell body. There are far more of the smaller dendrites than the larger axons and they are the key elements in the vast communications network that makes up your cortex.

DENDRITES

AXONS

Dendrites are much like "local" telephone connections, while axons are more analogous to the high capacity fiber-optic cable used for efficient long-distance transmissions. It's like having the vast Internet inside your head.

Put very simply, intelligence is a function of two factors —

(a) the number of functional neurons and, more important,

(b) the number of dendritic connections in your brain.

The first determines the size of your brain and its potential capacity. This does not vary a great deal between individuals. We all have the same basic potential. You have the same brain capacity and potential as Einstein or da Vinci. The real difference is in the number of connections between each neuron. This is where geniuses are made. Yes, MADE.

And it's never too late to increase your intelligence. Scientists are convinced that the ability to increase your brain's density by stimulating the growth of new dendritic connections continues throughout life: it does not diminish with age. You can make yourself into a genius.

When you challenge your mental capacity by learning new things and going beyond your intellectual comfort zone, you will be creating new dendrites and new connections to other parts of your brain. You will be increasing your intelligence! However, if you stop this process, as many of us do when we stop going to formal schools and find ourselves occupied with the pressures of work and family, we don't just stay the same.

You will actually lose brain density. You will lose dendritic mass and connections. You do lose intelligence.

The good news is that you do not lose the potential to recapture your previous level and even go beyond that. This may be difficult to believe, especially if you have tried to learn new things later in life and found it was much more difficult than when you were younger. Remember that it will take time to warm up your learning muscles and recondition yourself to learning new things if you've left that part of yourself inactive for a long time. If you haven't been pushing your brain for 5, 10, or 20 years, it is not realistic to expect that you will be able to jump right back into the swing of things and function like an experienced student.

But take heart! You haven't lost it. It's there inside you. No matter what your starting point is right now, you have the potential inside you to be smarter than ever before. It doesn't matter if you are a grade school drop-out or a Ph.D. You can do better than you ever dreamed of.

d. The two-sided brain

Within the most recently evolved of our three brains, the cortex, there is a distinct division of labor. Our major higher-brain functions such as speech, logical reasoning, and spatial analysis are each primarily focused in a particular area.

The most important division is the simple one between the left and right brain. Two scientists, Dr. Roger Sperry and Dr. Robert Ornstein, were awarded the Nobel Prize for their work in this area of research. Based on their work we know now that each side of the cortex is primarily responsible for characteristically different kinds of thinking.

LEFT BRAIN

The **left** side has responsibility for —

- logical reasoning and analysis,
- things that occur in sequences,
- numbers and mathematical ability,
- language and verbal skills,
- linear thinking, and
- rational and empirical thought.

The **right** side has responsibility for —

- creativity,
  - intuition,
    - music appreciation and rhythmic ability,
- imagination and daydreaming,
  - random, unordered thinking, and
- artistic senses (color, pattern, and spatial perceptions).

RIGHT BRAIN

As most of us know now, our thinking and learning patterns can be described in terms of which side dominates. In the typical way of our society, we often simplify this distinction to the point of triviality by calling people like engineers and lawyers very "left-brained" people, while artists and poets are "right-brained."

The reality of how our brain works is much more subtle than that. One side is dominant (90% left), but the other is very active and is not genetically or otherwise weaker, nor does it have less capacity.

The "problem" of left side dominance in most people has come about because of our society's emphasis on the concrete empirical values of the attributes of that left side. We have done our best to undervalue the characteristics of the right side of our brain and have seriously impaired our overall intelligence in the process. We have also assumed that such traits are hard-wired into us and therefore unchangeable, believing, for example, that the logical thinker cannot be creative and the artist cannot be expected to develop good linear management skills.

One of your major goals in improving your learning and studying is to bring more of your recessive side into play. Enhance the integration. Artists can think logically and linearly. Engineers and lawyers can be creative and intuitive.

e. Riding the brain waves

There are four basic states of mind in our daily lives and each has a different brain wave pattern. The best evidence we have of the bio-chemical — brain wave — activity is the variety of electrical impulses we can monitor and measure. This is a complex field of research, but a simplified explanation of the different brain wave patterns can tell us a lot about how to manage our studying more effectively.

BETA WAVES

Beta waves are indicative of the state of mind we normally associate with being awake and functioning in our world: communicating with others; walking or driving or otherwise moving about with purpose; analyzing, planning, and performing daily tasks.

This is the state in which we spend most of our lives. In this state we "get through" the day and accumulate achievements and a lot of stress. Our attention is constantly changing from one matter to another and back again. Our energy and focus is very fragmented as we try to deal with the thousands of things competing for our attention.

This state is vital if we are to function in our complex world, but it is hardly the best condition to be in when trying to concentrate on our studies. Yet it is the state of mind that most people are in when they sit down to do school work — and they do not try to change that state.

THETA WAVES

Theta waves are most evident when we are just about to drop off to sleep. They are also common in certain kinds of deep meditation.

DELTA WAVES

Delta waves are the "slowest" of the brain waves. These waves are what a scan would pick up when you are in a very deep sleep. And believe it or not, what happens during your sleeping state has important implications for how you plan your studying and how much you should study at one time (discussed in more detail in chapter 5).

ALPHA WAVES

Finally, *alpha waves* show up when you are fully awake, but in a very relaxed state — almost what could be called "alert meditation." There is very little stress in this state. The pathways between the various parts of your brain are clearest in this state, and your higher brain has its greatest access to other areas.

In this state of mind, you will experience the fastest understanding of information and the kind of inspiration that comes with letting your imagination help you connect things that never got connected before (realizing for the first time how similar the patterns of mathematics, music, and chess are, for example). There is also, in this state, the greatest likelihood that the information will find its way into long-term memory. Obviously, the state of mind that has a lot of alpha waves is where you want to be for optimum study performance.

When it comes to studying, it is important to literally get your brain on the right "wave length." Trying to study when you are in the everyday state of mind typical of that dominated by beta waves is very inefficient. You are battling many more enemies than just your textbooks.

Although it takes extra time to learn how to change your state of mind before beginning a study session, don't underestimate the importance of doing so. It is the change in approach that will bring you the most immediate results in study performance. It is so important that the next chapter in the book is devoted to introducing you to some of the key elements of preparing your "study state of mind" before you open a textbook.

f. Three modes of learning

Just as we have one side of our brain that is dominant, so too do we have a particular "mode" of learning that is our strongest. There are many different theories of how to identify and describe our possible learning styles. Some are very convoluted and detailed. The most accurate model seems to be the simplest.

The way in which we learn best can be easily slotted into one of three categories: visual learning, auditory learning, and kinesthetic learning. (These descriptions are simplified and are meant only as an introduction to the idea of different learning styles.)

1. Seeing

A *visual learner* is someone who learns best by seeing a representation of what he or she is studying, either in pictures, or written words, or an actual demonstration. Good visual learners tend to —

VISUAL LEARNER

- be strong readers (usually fast, but not always),
- be good spellers (usually because they can "see" the word),
- prefer, after a certain age, to read for themselves rather than have stories read to them,
- find it easier to remember things they see rather than just hear (such as having instructions written down rather than spoken, or using a map rather than listening to directions),
- doodle when thinking, talking on the phone, or during a meeting, and
- remember visual material presented in video tapes.

2. Hearing

AUDITORY LEARNER

An *auditory learner* is someone who learns best by hearing things. Such learners prefer hearing material in a lecture or classroom setting. Good auditory learners tend to —

- prefer talking to writing when describing something,
- prefer making a telephone call to writing a letter,
- become distracted by noise more than are visual learners,
- have a stronger sense for music than for visual arts such as painting, and
- remember what they hear more easily than what they see.

3. Doing

KINESTHETIC LEARNER

A *kinesthetic learner* is someone who learns best by actually doing it. Moving, touching, and experiencing something first-hand are often essential to this type of learner.

Good kinesthetic learners tend to —

- speak and write more slowly than the other two modalities of learners, but have confident fluid physical movements,
- use hand gestures more often,
- prefer hands-on learning to just seeing or hearing about something,
- have difficulty sitting still for extended periods when younger (not because of any "disorder," but because they are used to moving and exploring their world, and formal school discourages this),
- memorize things better and more easily when being physically active (such as walking around the room when reciting), and
- understand things better when they are acted out.

Research indicates that each of us has an initial preferred learning mode and that the distribution among the three modalities is roughly equal. In fact, the most common, by a small margin, is the kinesthetic and the least is visual. Yet our formal education system is set up to favor the visual, tolerate the auditory, and actively discourage (even punish) the kinesthetic.

Think about it. From the earliest grades the children who sit quietly and read or write are rewarded. Those who talk a lot and need the teacher to verbally explain things again and again are considered irritants. And the kids who fidget, move around, and cannot sit still are labelled "problems."

Just because one mode of learning tends to be stronger than the others, it does not mean that we cannot become adept at learning in other ways. The fidgety "problem" child can develop excellent ways of learning visually and auditorily. But that physical way of learning should not be undervalued or declared a deficit of some kind. The more we find ways to study and learn that force us to use all three modalities, the more effective we become in the same amount of time.

g. Seven kinds of intelligence

Theories of multiple intelligences in our brains have been with us for centuries. The model based on the latest clinical research and actual scans of brain activity is that pioneered by Dr. Howard Gardner of Harvard University. Gardner has identified seven distinctly different intelligences within each person. Others have tried to extend his list by separating out some characteristics that Gardner has grouped together. But for the purpose of this book and developing a basic understanding that will help you study smarter, let's just look at Gardner's list of seven.

1. Linguistic

Talent with language and the ability to write well are common characteristics of linguistic intelligence. The great writers and orators of history have been especially strong linguistically. People who love to read a lot or seem to have "the gift of the gab" are strong in linguistic intelligence.

2. Mathematical/logical

The ability to think logically and be proficient in numerical tasks are big components of mathematical/logical intelligence. Most abstract linear kinds of reasoning require this kind of intelligence. Any career that depends on numbers requires strength in mathematical and logical thinking (science, engineering, accountancy, and statistics, for example).

As Gardner points out, these first two are those most prized and rewarded by the formal school system. Students who have highly developed intelligences of these kinds are often the most successful in their studies and perform best on

Reading is to the mind what exercise is to the body. It is wholesome and bracing for the mind to have its faculties kept in stretch.

Augustus Hare

The mathematician has reached the highest rung on the ladder of human thought.

Havelock Ellis

one- or two-dimensional tests such as I.Q. and S.A.T. Their performance will usually result in acceptance to good universities and colleges. However, success when they leave the formal school setting will often depend on one of the other intelligences.

For example, a surgeon will rely on linguistic and logical intelligences to get into medical school and acquire the body of knowledge necessary to graduate. But it will be the bodily/kinesthetic/physical intelligence that will give that surgeon the skills necessary to be a success after initial medical training.

Mathematical and linguistic intelligences are essential to success in business school. However, it is the highly developed interpersonal and intrapersonal intelligences that will determine success in the business world.

3. Musical

The capacity to understand, appreciate, and create music characterizes this underrated intelligence. Great musicians and composers obviously have musical intelligence in a very enhanced form, but everyone has it even if he or she has usually thought of himself or herself as "unmusical."

It is your musical intelligence that helps you keep rhythm. It also keeps that annoying tune running around in your head. When you memorize a poem, it will be your linguistic intelligence that helps you remember the words and the rhyme scheme, but it is your musical intelligence that comes into play when the rhythm or meter of the poem triggers your memory.

4. Visual/spatial

Visual/spatial intelligence is most often associated with artistic ability. While it is true that painters and sculptors have a particularly well-developed visual intelligence, this intelligence is also a major part of the ability that makes architects, interior designers, pilots, bush trackers, and city planners successful.

In addition to being active when an artist physically *makes* a picture, visual/spatial intelligence is active when you see things in your mind's eye or internally visualize. It takes good visual/spatial intelligence to use a map or plan a garden.

It is also a key component of a highly efficient memory (as you will see in chapter 5). If someone asked you to itemize from

The principles of logic and metaphysics are true simply because we never allow them to be anything else.

A.J. Ayer

Music is the arithmetic of sounds as optics is the geometry of light.

Claude Debussy

Art is ruled uniquely by the imagination.

Benedetto Croce

memory all the things in your living room, you would depend on your visual intelligence to recall those items.

5. Physical

Physical intelligence is also referred to as bodily or kinesthetic intelligence. It includes obvious things such as athletic ability and body movement, but it also encompasses skills such as the manual dexterity of a carpenter, surgeon, or weaver.

Being good with your hands means your physical intelligence is well developed. Not only is this intelligence valuable in its own right and toward its own ends, but you can also heighten your use of other, more academically oriented intelligences if you incorporate some physicality into your learning.

Dancing is the loftiest, the most moving, the most beautiful of the arts, because it is no mere translation or abstraction from life; it is life itself.

Havelock Ellis

6. Interpersonal

Interpersonal intelligence is social talent — being good with other people. Skill or innate ability to make people feel comfortable and at ease around you is a very valuable intelligence in our highly interdependent global society, and an ability to get along well and communicate with others is one of the most highly rewarded skills in our society.

This talent is prevalent in people who work in sales, high-level negotiation and diplomacy, and motivational speaking. The best teachers and managers are "gifted" in this way, or they have made a conscious effort to develop their interpersonal intelligence.

Be nice to people on your way up because you'll meet 'em on your way down.

Wilson Mizner

7. Intrapersonal

The capacity for self-analysis and the ability to examine your own behavior is an intelligence which Gardner calls intrapersonal. Introspection and a talent for understanding your own feelings is evidence of the kind of intelligence that is key to setting goals, planning the future, daydreaming, and accessing your intuitive nature. You cannot improve in the future if you have no understanding of who and what you are at the moment.

The unexamined life is not worth living.

Socrates

This wide variety of intelligences is present in all of us. Think of da Vinci — scientist, artist, linguist, inventor. His range is not beyond each of us (although his level may be).

The first step is to recognize the reality. The second step is to do something about it, and one of the best ways to do so is to incorporate this notion into the things you do to learn and study.

It has been proven that if you use more than one or two intelligences in your studying, you will learn more, learn faster, and will be more likely to recall the information for the exam and even years later. It will become part of you.

You may want to read in detail Gardner's two books on the subject: *Frames of Mind* and *Multiple Intelligences*. Also, a more accessible book, written for the general public, is *7 Kinds of Smart: Identifying and Developing Your Many Intelligences*, by Thomas Armstrong.

h. So what?

What does all this have to do with your learning ability and your need to develop good study skills RIGHT NOW?

The answer to that holds the key to studying SMARTER, not HARDER. If you are going to take the time and effort to work on your study skills, doesn't it make sense to develop a toolbox of skills that contains things that will make the most of your incredible potential? Build better skills and capacity for learning in the future? A future that will involve you in learning for the rest of your life?

If it takes the same time and effort to get As as it does to just pass, wouldn't you want to get As? That's what this chapter has been all about. You learn something about how the brain and intelligence really works, and the rest of the book makes more sense. You will understand what underlies the hints and exercises throughout the chapters.

The next three chapters take things a step further. In them you will discover the most important stage of learning (preparation) and find out some vital information about how memory works.

4.

Preparation: The most important part of learning

a. Preparing yourself to learn is the most important part of learning

The first step toward realizing your potential genius and becoming a better learner is to recognize the vital role played by preparation. I don't mean the actual details of preparation of the material for an exam, but the extensive preparation you need to do before you even open your book to study or enter the lecture hall.

This is probably a new concept for you. Most people "just sit down and do it," but that is why most people experience only a fraction of the learning success of which they are capable.

As an example, take a fairly typical student who is going to attempt to study. This student sits down at the kitchen table with textbooks and notes for three subjects in a pile in front of her. The radio is blaring news, commercials, and music. Roommates or family members are passing through the kitchen to chat, get something from the refrigerator, or prepare a meal.

The student takes the first book off the pile, opens to read the assigned chapter, and stares at the first page. But little is sinking in. Things haven't been going too well in this class and the stress of that surfaces very quickly as soon as she even thinks about the subject, let alone tries to study it. And there is the additional stress of others' expectations and demands. If she doesn't pass the next test, her parents are going to cause her a lot of grief. And there's even more stress because there is a mid-term exam tomorrow in another of her courses, the textbook for which is at the bottom of the pile, and she hasn't even started studying for that one.

It all seems impossible. She can't remember what she read 15 seconds ago. Maybe she's just too dumb. Maybe she should just give up and go watch TV.

Does that sound familiar? Do you know anyone who has ever been in this situation? Perhaps the person you know like this is very close to you? Perhaps that person is reading this book with you at this very moment?

Our hypothetical student is at war with several of the deadliest enemies of good studying:

- Fear
- Stress
- Distractions
- Low self-esteem
- Overwhelmed
- No plan of attack
- Poor concentration
- Low level of will power
- No will to succeed

Most of these enemies can be dealt with by good preparation before you begin to study. The strategies in this chapter will get you started on this neglected aspect of learning. If you follow these directions, you will experience dramatic positive results almost immediately. But the real payoff comes when you do these things day after day after day.

If you do nothing else that's outlined in this book, you will still see a 100% to 400% improvement in all aspects of your studying if you do what's recommended in this chapter and DO NOT STOP DOING IT! The strategies are that powerful!

b. What are you trying to achieve with preparation?

You now know from chapter 3 that you certainly have the brain power to learn anything you want, and it's clear that lack of intelligence is NOT the reason most people have difficulty studying. And chapters 8 to 14 can give enough skills, tips, and hints so that you have the tools to be successful, so it's clear that lack of know-how won't hold you back.

But all your intelligence and a toolbox of study skills will be useless if you don't prepare properly.

Your goal in the preparation phase of studying is to create the optimum state of mind for learning. You want to be confident, enthusiastic, relaxed, calm, focused, and alert. This is what advocates of accelerated learning call the "resourceful state of mind." You will feel a unique kind of relaxed alertness that lets you use the amazing power of relaxed concentration that comes from activating the alpha type of brain waves we talked about in chapter 3.

There are five basic elements to this process:

- Preparing your learning environment
- Relaxing to control your anxiety and stress
- Pumping up your self-esteem
- Sharpening your focus
- Activating your brain for the subject at hand

c. Preparing a place to study

Believe it or not, the most effective way to battle the problems of distractions, poor concentration, and low self-esteem is to improve your learning environment. No matter how hard you try, you cannot learn with the radio or TV on. You cannot learn at the kitchen table, at the living room coffee table, on your bed, or at the campus coffee shop. It won't happen. You may struggle through, but you will be functioning at a level far below your potential just because of where you choose to study.

33

1. Find a study place

You must establish a place that is only for studying. Don't kid yourself: the majority of concentration problems come from distractions that occur because you study in the wrong place.

Select a place that is quiet, comfortable, and relaxing. You want to create a space that has associations related only to studying. When you sit down at this place, the subconscious messages that come into your brain tell you that this is where you study, and do nothing else but study.

Not your bed. The subliminal messages from that place are SLEEP. That's not an association you want to battle when you're trying to be focused and alert.

Not the kitchen table (or any other place in your home or residence that is a common area). Not only are the associations in that place related to food, but they tend to be in places where people congregate and do other things. It's a people area, not a study area. Don't expect to get much work done here.

Not in the living room. Like the kitchen, there are too many distractions and competing associations and temptations here (such as the TV).

Not in the cafeteria or coffee shop. That's where your friends gather; that's where people around you are talking and laughing. Those places are specifically designed for relaxation, not work.

The best place is a desk in your bedroom, or in the basement, or somewhere relatively free of distractions and competing associations. Try the library or an empty classroom.

If you haven't established such a study place, do it now before you try any of the other preparation techniques. Your study place is the foundation to your study program.

Once you have your primary study space all set up, your next task is to decide on a secondary place. It's important to have a back-up. One of the best reasons for procrastination is looking for an alternative place to study when you can't use your primary space for some reason. Wandering around trying to find a place that feels right wastes a lot of time. This is especially important if you like to study at school or on campus. If someone is in your usual spot, what do you do? Go immediately to your predetermined back-up and get to work.

The other great value of having one or two alternatives is that they become familiar and you expend less energy trying to fend off the distractions that are inevitable when you are in a new space.

2. Make it comfortable

Studying is primarily a sedentary activity. You sit in a chair for long periods and there's no way to avoid that. Therefore, first and foremost, it is essential to have a comfortable chair. You do not want the kind of comfort you feel when you lounge on a couch or stretch out on your bed. What you need is the kind of comfort and body support that will let you sit for up to an hour without any pain and discomfort to get in the way of concentration.

Your chair should be well padded on the seat and back. The back should give firm, consistent support to your back and the seat should give the same to your thighs. The ideal height is that which allows your feet to be placed easily on the soles, easing most of the pressure on the ankle and knee joints.

It is worth every penny you spend to buy a proper chair. It is a wise investment in your learning future. If you really cannot afford a new chair, try to make what you have as comfortable as possible. A small pillow on the seat and a blanket or down jacket draped over the back can transform that awful wooden library chair into one that becomes a true assistant in your learning.

You also need to consider the quality of the air in your study place. Air, or rather the oxygen in air, is literally the fuel that your brain requires to do its work. Remember that the brain constitutes approximately 2% of the body's weight, but it uses 20% of the oxygen you take in.

You want the temperature to be properly balanced. Extremes of hot and cold cause distractions of discomfort. If perfect temperature is unlikely, it's better to be in a place that is too cool rather than too warm. It's easy to get warmer by putting on warmer clothes, and cooler air keeps you alert. Air that is too warm makes you drowsy and robs you of your ability to focus for any extended period.

Fresh air is vital. Stale, dead air means your brain is getting substandard fuel.

3. Check the lighting

Natural light is better than artificial light. If artificial light is unavoidable, incandescent light is better than fluorescent. The latter is the worst for eye strain and, therefore, an impairment to effective studying.

Make sure you have enough light. Don't be fooled by the romantic image of the scholar toiling in the dark room with only one faint candle or lamp over his or her desk. Chances are that scholar has either dozed off or is slowly going blind.

Always have at least two light sources in your study area. Not only does this help give you sufficient total light, but it will help reduce eye strain. If you have a good light over your desk but the rest of the room is in total darkness, your eye muscles will have to work extra hard to adjust to the extremes of light and blackness when they wander. Yes, your eyes will wander when you study — even with good focus and concentration, your eyes will move throughout the room.

You can give your eyes a break by having sufficient light from different sources so that when they shift they are not struggling to deal with sudden darkness and then sudden bright light.

4. Have everything ready

The best preparation for good work tomorrow is to do good work today.

Elbert Hubbard

One of the most effective ways to waste time is to spend it gathering all the study materials and other little things before you open a book. It's easy to fool yourself into thinking you are accomplishing something useful while sitting at your desk and looking busy. But it's useless activity.

Your study time is for studying. Before the clock starts, make certain you have everything you need right in front of you: all the pens, pencils, rulers, erasers, highlighters, and all your textbooks, notebooks, and other reading material.

5. Post a lot of positive messages around the space

One of the major distractions to consistent focus and concentration is the nagging doubt you may have about your ability. Years of struggling to succeed but coming up short can take its toll on self-esteem. You need to build up that aspect of yourself — just as an athlete builds up strength and endurance.

This takes time and it takes a plan. Throughout this book you will find many different ways to develop strong confidence in yourself and your ability to learn anything. When it comes to your physical learning environment, you can enhance your self-esteem by surrounding yourself with positive messages.

Pictures of yourself with family and friends are good to have around, especially if they depict you getting hugged. Don't laugh; it works. Have any awards, trophies, certificates, or testimonials on your wall or bulletin board. Put up motivational posters, quotes, or snappy reminders of the positive value of what you are doing and just how vast your potential really is. Use some of the quotes and slogans in this book.

The point is to create a positive mental and emotional environment in which you will study. Surrounding yourself with things carrying a positive message will not have an immediate, dramatic impact. By themselves they won't do much. But it's amazing how powerful they can be as "booster shots" when your mind wanders and you begin to have doubts.

Positive self-image and confidence in your learning ability must come from within, but just imagine how much better you will feel when your homework starts to get you down and you look up to see something uplifting in front of your face — something in big bold letters that says:

I can Learn ANYTHING
I am a FABULOUS Learner

Isn't that more helpful than a blank wall and your secret fears of inadequacy? If there isn't anyone around to give you a pat on the back, set things up so you can give one to yourself.

6. Enrich your environment

It is very important that your study place be somewhere you enjoy going. If it's pleasant and inviting, it's less likely that you will avoid going there to do your work. Factors like comfort, light, quiet, positive associations, and inspiring messages all around it are key.

You can do many other little things to make it even better:

- Flowers and plants provide some brightness and natural color, providing a substantial calming effect.

- Study at desks and work surfaces that have natural wood grains.
- Use an air purifier or humidifier to help if there are air quality problems.
- Use soft-foam ear plugs to help block out distracting noise without undue pressure on your ears.

Once you have your physical work environment ready for studying, you are ready to begin preparing your inner world for top learning performance.

d. Preparing your mind for studying

1. Define your goals and objectives

Having a defined objective, or series of objectives, for each study session is essential for success and mind preparation. Chapter 8 contains a detailed discussion of goal setting and the characteristics your short-term goals — such as those for a single study session — should have. The best study goals are always —

- **realistic** for the time allowed (i.e., what can you reasonably accomplish in one hour?),

- **concrete** and **specific** (e.g., read 11 pages of psychology, NOT read "some" psychology; or do 18 math problems, NOT do "some" math),

- **verifiable** (i.e., you can tell when you're done),

- **significant** and **rewardable** (e.g., one chapter of history warrants a reward of going to a movie), and

- **relevant** to your priorities (e.g., finishing chapter 5 in biology because it will be on the test tomorrow is more relevant at the moment than doing your English assignment that isn't due until next week).

Knowing ahead of time exactly what it is you hope to accomplish each time you sit down to study does several helpful things for your efficiency and mind power:

- It helps overcome procrastination by eliminating the time wasted by trying to decide what to work on.
- It helps keep you on task while you're working; having a specific objective makes it harder to rationalize quitting before you've achieved it.

The point of having an open mind, like having an open mouth, is to close it on something solid.

G.K. Chesterton

- It generates a feeling of progress and success when you set and complete a concrete goal. This kind of success can easily begin to cascade and you find you love seeing tasks getting crossed off your to-do list (more about to-do lists in chapters 8 and 9).
- It helps break large, daunting tasks into more easily managed chunks of small tasks.

Never sit down to "do some studying." That is a bad habit that can quickly degenerate into doing no studying because the total amount of work seems overwhelming and you feel out of control.

2. Plan a lot of activities

Remember, you want to use as much of your brain as possible. While you certainly have a dominant or preferred learning style, you must go beyond that in order to become the genius-level learner you want to be.

One of your objectives in preparation should be to plan study activities that are purposely designed to engage and stimulate as many of your different intelligences as possible. Therefore, plan to read, listen, review, sing, walk around, read quietly, make notes, draw learning maps, etc. There will be many different suggestions throughout other chapters in the book. While you're still getting used to doing activities that are different from those of your comfortable learning style, it helps to consciously plan them so that you don't slip back into old habits too often.

3. Prepare your state of mind — and body

Stress and anxiety are two significant inhibitors of effective studying and learning. Remember from the previous chapter that when we experience fear and threats to our safety, the reptilian brain dominates our physiological and psychological responses. Any negative stress triggers this reaction and it tends to block access to the higher brain functions.

Stress is normal, but so is the receding of that stress so we can rest, relax, and recover. The nature of the pressures placed on us by society, our families, and ourselves means that we are constantly tense and putting inordinate stress on our physical, psychological, emotional, and spiritual systems. Medical experts are now realizing that this constant stress results in hormonal imbalances, impaired immune systems, and other related maladies such as heart disease.

Obviously you can't be the best possible learner in this state of mind and body. If society won't change to allow you to relax and recover from stress, then the next best thing for you to do is to learn how to do it for yourself. Learn to relax with proper breathing and muscle manipulation, and your learning will improve.

Remember, your goal in preparation is to achieve a "relaxed alertness" before you attempt to learn anything new. As Colin Rose, an early popularizer of accelerated learning, describes it, you want to begin your study session as if it were a concert — you are feeling calm but excited with the anticipation of what is to come. You are relaxed and ready to just let it happen.

(a) Breathing

Breathing in is taking in supplies; breathing out, slowly and deeply, spreads them throughout the body.

Taisen Deshimaru,
The Zen Way to the Martial Arts

One thing all living human beings have in common is breathing. Breath is the essence of life. Breathing is so automatic that we never think much about it until something gets in the way of our breathing. It is so simple, yet most people do it wrong!

Obviously, if you're alive, then you are breathing well enough to get by, but you could be doing much better. And it is important to do better because your brain is very sensitive to the quality of your breathing.

The brain accounts for approximately 2% of the body's weight, but it uses around 20% of the oxygen you take in. The better you are at providing the brain with its basic fuel, the better the performance you will get out of that engine.

The biggest breathing mistake people make is that they breathe too rapidly and too shallowly — ordinarily 15 to 22 times per minute. Breathing that quickly means that you could be using as little as one-sixth of your lungs' intake and distribution capacities.

It is possible to train yourself to take only five to six calm, full breaths in a minute. The overall result of this kind of breathing will be increased general health, improved alertness, an enhanced immune system, greatly reduced anxiety, and a surprising change for the better in your level of concentration.

The basic principles are to inhale slowly and deeply, filling your lungs as completely as possible, and then to exhale the same way, expelling all the waste products and distributing the oxygen you've retained. This kind of breathing also works the diaphragm and, consequently, massages several internal organs.

Look at Exercise #1 for a full explanation of how to achieve "natural breathing."

(b) Muscle relaxation

Stress not only influences breathing, but it also puts a lot of strain on our muscles. It is very common for people to deal with their anxiety by clenching their jaw muscles (resulting in tension headaches), tensing their neck and shoulder muscles (causing neck and upper back aches), or sitting forward constantly (causing lower back pain).

Obviously, this kind of tension is not conducive to productive studying. Therefore, a good program of muscle relaxation is an important part of preparation to learning. There are many different ways to accomplish effective relaxation of tense, knotted muscles. One of the best is a simple series of contractions and releases, described in Exercise #2.

(c) Visualization

Visualization is another excellent preparation technique. It uses the same basic patterning and brain processes as memory. There is a direct correlation between activated memories and the physical body. A memory that evokes feelings of fear, anxiety, or pain will immediately change your heart rate, skin temperature, and brain wave patterns. A happy, joyous memory will affect the same things, but in a positive way. Each kind of memory will stimulate an electro-chemical reaction in your brain.

As a simple example, close your eyes and imagine a lemon in front of you. Imagine taking a sharp kitchen knife and slicing the lemon in half. Can you see the juice oozing out onto the table? Can you smell that wonderful lemon scent as it's released from the fruit? Take one of the halves and bring it up to your mouth. Open your mouth and hold it poised to bite over the lemon half. Don't bite just yet. Now bite down hard into the fruit and rind. Can you feel the juice explode over your tongue and taste buds? Does it squirt down around your gums and flow to the back of your mouth? Can you feel the sting of the concentrated liquid released from the rind? Do your nostrils fill with an even more powerful lemon aroma?

See? At what point did your mouth start to water and you could actually experience some of the sensations: the taste, the smell, the sting? Your mind with its associations is amazingly powerful. It can make your body react when there is nothing present but your imagination.

Visualization becomes a positive study technique when it is used to maximize positive feelings and reduce negative ones. You can learn to bring up good memories on demand, using visualization of the past. You can also learn to use images of how you want things to be, using visualization of the future. The positive feelings and the brain physiology that underlies them are the same for each.

If you have difficulty closing your eyes and conjuring up sharp visual images, don't despair. Do not fall back on the claim that you simply aren't good at that kind of thing. It takes practice. Everyone has this ability, but some have used it more than others. Give it a try.

There are dozens, even hundreds, of guided visualization and imagery techniques. Exercise #3 includes four simple ones you can use in your study preparation. The first two are good for calming yourself if you are particularly anxious or upset. They will help calm your nerves and still your racing brain.

The third and fourth techniques are more motivational and are useful for pumping up your self-confidence just before trying to study one of your more difficult subjects. All four are useful training exercises for increasing your visualization ability, which is a vital for memory and exam preparation.

(d) Positive self-image

Positive feelings about yourself are vital to your study success. As you can see, they can be a key component to effective visualization. You boost your self-esteem in many ways: planning for success, imagining success, building on success, sharing your gifts.

But since one of the ways you can sabotage yourself is by listening to the nagging voice of doubt, you also must pay attention to the necessity of training that inner voice to be more positive.

The process of working on your inner voice is usually called "affirmations." It is a simple pattern of positive self-talk that

EXERCISE #1
NATURAL BREATHING TECHNIQUE

Step 1: ⟶ Inhale through your nose, but do not expand your chest.

That's the biggest mistake people make. If your chest is expanding, you are breathing shallowly and actually constricting your lungs. When inhaling, your chest should remain unchanged, but you should expand your belly. Imagine there is a balloon in your tummy and your job is to blow as much air as possible into it. Inhalation should take six seconds. (The average person inhales for only two seconds.) This will bring much more oxygen into your body.

In the beginning, this step will feel weird. What you are doing is pushing your diaphragm and abdomen in such a way that the space inside your chest cavity increases, allowing more room for your lungs. It's much easier to fill your lungs with air this way.

Step 2: ⟶ Pause.

The first time you try this kind of breathing you will discover that you feel a little out of breath. That's normal. If you feel that way, you may want to skip the pauses after inhaling for now. When you are more comfortable with the basic pattern of inhaling and exhaling, begin to insert the pauses.

One of the purposes of the pause is to exercise your diaphragm and internal muscles. It helps train your breathing apparatus. Once you become comfortable with the inhaling and exhaling pattern, add the pauses.

Step 3: ⟶ Exhale slowly and evenly for six seconds.

This is done by relaxing the abdomen and allowing the lungs to expel the air. The chest may expand slightly.

When breathing this way during normal activity, you will want to exhale through the nose. When you're doing it as a conscious exercise to train your breathing or to prepare yourself for studying, it's best to breathe out through your mouth — gently, not forcefully.

Step 4: ⟶ Pause before beginning to inhale again.

Beginner pattern

Using the natural breathing technique, take ten full, deep breaths. Inhale for six seconds, then exhale for six seconds. Do not consciously pause between each inhale or exhale. If you find difficulty with the six-second cycle, find one that is comfortable for you (perhaps three seconds) and gradually work your way up to six seconds.

Set aside five minutes so you can do this three times a day. If possible, practice your breathing while sitting comfortably in a chair with your feet flat on the floor and your arms resting loosely in your lap.

Focus your attention on your breathing. Visualize the expansion and contraction of your lungs. Imagine the increased volume of oxygen that you're taking in is going directly to your brain and feeding those hungry neurons.

While doing this exercise, even for the first time, you will increase the use of your lungs' capacity from 15% to 80%. You will get even more efficient with practice; with daily practice, breathing like this will become automatic.

Intermediate pattern

Once you feel comfortable with the beginner pattern, move on to an intermediate pattern. Do everything the same as the beginner's, but add two wrinkles.

Try doing the pauses between the inhalation and exhalation cycles. For instance, you would inhale, hold for a count of four, and then exhale. Hold for another count of four, and then inhale, and so on.

The key is not to rush the breathing in or out after the pause. Try very hard to do the same calm, even, full breath each time. If that's too hard, reduce the pause time. Work your way up to a pause of ten seconds.

At this level, focus your attention on the air you breathe in. Imagine that it is sparkling energy that will fill you with vitality and genius. As you breathe in, picture this energy filling your lungs completely. As you exhale, visualize all the good energy being distributed from your lungs to your brain and all other areas of your body, and imagine that what you expel is stress and negative feelings.

Advanced Pattern

Advanced breathing techniques are a fascinating study, but they are more relevant for meditation and deep reflection. The first two patterns are those most appropriate for preparing yourself to study.

If you are interested in more in-depth training of your breathing technique, check at your local colleges and recreation centers for instruction. Advanced breathing technique is an element in many martial arts, but you will also find it in yoga, tai chi, and qi gong (a traditional Chinese healing and health discipline).

EXERCISE #2
MUSCLE RELAXATION

Step 1: ——————————————————————→ sit

Sit as described in Exercise #1, or lie down in a comfortable position.

Step 2: ————————————————→ breathe

Go through one cycle of ten breaths without pauses
(beginner pattern — see Exercise #1).

Step 3: ——————————————→ tense

Tense your neck muscles as hard as you can. Clench them hard.

Step 4: ——————————————→ release

Slowly release the muscle tension. Don't do it quickly. Instead, you should gently
let go. Let all the muscles go as loose and limp as possible. Imagine all the pain
and stress is draining from your neck muscles, out of your finger tips, and out of
your body.

Step 5: ———————————→ next muscle group

Next, do the same thing with your facial muscles. Scrunch them as hard as
possible. Then slowly relax them while all the tension flows out of your body.

Step 6: ——————————————→ continue

Continue this pattern until you have done it with all your muscle groups: neck,
face, shoulders, back, chest, abdomen, buttocks, thighs, calves, ankles, and toes.

Try to isolate each muscle group. For example, when crunching your neck and
shoulders, try not to tense your arms or any other part of your body.

To stay alert and be ready for a session of studying, you should do this exercise
with your eyes open and not take a lot of time with it — say two to three minutes.

This is a fairly simple, standard muscle relaxation technique. If you want to
relax more, perhaps even fall asleep, do it lying down with your eyes closed.
Spend more time on each muscle group, and as you relax the tension, imagine
yourself getting heavier, looser, and sleepier. If you have difficulty sleeping and
that is getting in the way of productive studying, try this pattern.

EXERCISE #3
VISUALIZATION TECHNIQUES

1. "My quiet place"

Find a quiet place with as few distractions as possible. Begin by sitting comfortably and take at least ten natural breaths using the beginner pattern (Exercise #1).

Close your eyes gently and imagine the inside of your eye lids as a movie screen. Picture a physical setting that makes you feel calm and relaxed. Where do you feel most peaceful? A sunny clearing in the woods? In a canoe on a still lake at sunset? Lying in the afternoon prairie sun in the autumn? In a book-lined study with classical music playing in the background?

Select the setting that gives you the strongest feeling of tranquility. It can be a place you have actually been to, or you can construct the entire scene from your imagination.

Now sharpen your image of this place by using all your senses to provide reality. Imagine the colors of the sunset. Can you feel the warmth coming up from the prairie earth? What smells are coming from the early morning dew?

Sharpen the images still further with more specific detail. What kind of trees are you surrounded by? Are they old-growth or young trees? Is the clearing near a lake or stream? Can you hear the rushing water? If there is classical music, what kind is it? If it's Bach, what is the actual piece? Is it Orchestral Suite no. 3 in D Major? Get as detailed as you can.

As you work on the clarity of the vision, pay attention to your feelings while in this place. Focus on your sense of calm and tranquil restfulness. Let all the elements of the scene wash over you. Open your awareness to the quiet and peace surrounding you.

Save your image and come back to it. Add detail. Change characteristics if you like. Practice evoking your quiet place on demand.

2. "My sanctuary"

This exercise is much like the first, but the focus is primarily an interior space rather than an outdoor setting. It is a modern version of an ancient exercise devised by Da Mo, who is reputed to have brought the foundations of kung fu from India to China. Like the first exercise, this exercise helps develop the sensory imagination and create a place of refuge for you. It is a place where you are in complete control.

Find a quiet place with as few distractions as possible. Begin by sitting comfortably and take at least ten natural breaths using the beginner pattern (Exercise #1).

Close your eyes gently and imagine the inside of your eye lids as a movie screen. Picture a remote mountain that is tall and solid, but not so imposing that it is fearful. Imagine yourself seeing this mountain from a few hundred meters away, with a winding path leading to its base. As you walk along the path, you begin to make out an opening at the base of the mountain. It is the mouth of a cave. When you walk right up to it, you realize that there is a large door closing off the entrance. You have the only key and you use it to open the door.

You enter the cave and your eyes adjust quickly. Rather than a cold, damp, depressing place, your first impression of your cave is of a solid, safe sanctuary bathed in warm light from torches lighting the vaulted hallway. The short hallway leads into a huge cathedral-style cavern with three inviting entryways: one straight ahead and one each to the right and left.

Through the arch to the left is a research center filled with books and a computer system that looks like it belongs on the *Starship Enterprise*. This is where you can find the answer to any problem you may have. There are always answers (although not always ones you want to face), and this is your mental research institute for finding them.

EXERCISE #3 — Continued

On the right-hand side is a transportation center filled with portals that will let you travel to anywhere and to any time. You can go places you've never been, revisit favorite special places, or talk with anyone you please (e.g., Einstein or a long-lost love).

Straight ahead of you is your living chamber. You can construct this place in any way you choose. Make it as simple or elaborate as you want. Some who use this technique prefer an austere compartment. Others may start out that way, but soon they have developed it into a sumptuous mansion with all the luxuries. It's up to you. This is your sanctuary.

These are the basic features of the sanctuary visualization. You will find that the longer you work at this, the more personal and detailed the images become. Since the sanctuary is meant to be a place of refuge and contemplation for you and only you, make it any way you want. Let your imagination run wild: Put in a pool for swimming laps. Put in station guards outside the cave entrance (no one is allowed inside but you). Put in a skylight. Have fun.

3. "I can do it!" — version A

In this visualization, you develop the ability to quickly recall your past successes. Select an event from your personal history when you felt terrific about yourself and your accomplishments: you aced your biology test, or you were the hero for your softball team, or you finally passed your piano exam, or your painting received an honorable mention, or your lover went crazy over the birthday present you gave him or her. Whatever it was that made you feel on top of the world, grab onto it with your memory.

Find a quiet place with as few distractions as possible. Begin by sitting comfortably and take at least ten natural breaths using the beginner pattern (Exercise #1).

Close your eyes gently and imagine the inside of your eye lids as a movie screen. Remember the pride and sense of accomplishment. How did it make you feel inside? Did you believe you

49

were a good, worthwhile person? Did you have a sense of strength? Did it give you a feeling that you could do more than you thought you might be capable of?

Practice sharpening your recall of the feelings you experienced during that time. Replay it in your mind so that all the images are clear.

Each time you do that, you release a certain kind of chemical in your brain that helps program you for success. If you do this immediately before a study session, you can easily double your retention and learning power — just by feeling good about yourself. Use your past experience to convince yourself that you can do it. You can do anything!

4. "I can do it!" — version B

In this exercise, you will be developing similar memories of success, but this time the images are of the future. You will be able to feel the exhilaration of success when you have achieved your goal.

Find a quiet place with as few distractions as possible. Begin by sitting comfortably and take at least ten natural breaths using the beginner pattern (Exercise #1).

Close your eyes gently and imagine the inside of your eye lids as a movie screen. Begin by recalling the success sensations from something that actually happened to you. Let those feelings wash over you and fill you up. Let yourself get excited.

Now, while those good feelings are fresh, imagine yourself at the end of the exam for which you are studying. How will it feel to have answered all the questions correctly? How good will you feel about yourself just before the exam, knowing you're fully prepared and ready for anything? What will it feel like to get your first A? Or another A? You can do it!

plants seeds in your subconscious mind about your capabilities. Sounds a little too simplistic, doesn't it?

Parents know that a constant barrage of negative feedback will severely damage a child's self-esteem. Even an off-hand, good-natured reference to a child as a "dummy," or a remark made quickly in a flash of anger or frustration, such as "you stupid idiot, how could you do that? Don't you know any better?" can have devastating repercussions if it happens often enough. Eventually, the child, and later the adult, develops a negative self-image and begins to believe the things said.

Well, if negative self-talk can be so powerful, it can certainly be countered and overcome by its positive corollary. Positive self-talk is simple but effective — especially when combined with other study prep techniques.

As a starting point, write out a list of ten positive affirmations that are relevant to you as a learner. They do not need to be complex or profound. Here are some good examples:

AFFIRMATIONS

- I can learn anything.
- My brain is powerful.
- I will be prepared and confident for every exam.
- I am a powerful learner.
- I am relaxed and alert and ready to learn.
- There is nothing I can't learn and master.
- I have genius potential.
- With practice, I will always get better.

Now you should write your own. Always be definitive and confident in your statements, not cautious or understated. Don't say "maybe" or "probably" — it will only undermine the affirmation process. Also, always write and say them in the first person, using pronouns such as "I," "me," and "my." It is much more significant to your subconscious if you say "My brain is powerful" rather than "The brain is a powerful thing." The point is to make your affirmations personal.

The way to plant these beliefs about yourself deeply into your mind so they become part of you is to constantly repeat them to yourself. You won't feel the effect immediately, but it does come — and sooner than you may expect. Try not to think of this as a quick fix, but rather as a permanent change in your life. Repeat your affirmations five to ten times at least twice a day at regular times — when you're in the shower, or going for a run, or driving to school, or washing the dishes, for example. Make it a regular part of your life.

If repeating your affirmations is also a regular part of what you do just before opening your books to study, you will develop a strong mental association between the good things you are saying about yourself and the process of studying. It is amazing what a powerful effect that will have on your learning.

(e) Music

When it comes to learning, music can be magic. The pioneering work of Dr. Georgi Lozanov, a Bulgarian medical doctor and neuroscientist, has become the foundation of the movement variously referred to as Accelerated Learning, Quantum Learning, SuperLearning, Accelerative Learning, and CyberLearning. What Dr. Lozanov discovered was that certain kinds of music, used in specific ways, had the power to accelerate the learning process to unheard-of levels.

Music cannot be expressed in words, not because it is vague but because it is more precise than words.

Felix Mendelssohn

There have been seemingly outlandish claims for learning methods based on Lozanov's theories, such as learning and retaining up to 500 new foreign language words in a session and becoming functional in a new language within a week. However, as more scientists and teachers are able to replicate and build on his work, more and more educators are seeing astonishing possibilities of his approach. It is becoming more common in the mainstream of society, and hundreds of organizations are using training techniques based on his theories, including AT&T, General Motors, the U.S. Department of Defense, Hilton Hotels, and UNESCO.

Lozanov discovered the power of music to break down mental blocks to learning by relaxing the student. He also found that certain kinds of music were highly conducive to harmonizing the body's brain wave patterns, heart rhythms, and basic electro-chemical functions.

Lozanov was not the first to discover the mind-music connection, but his innovation was to develop a comprehensive learning system around scientific verification of this idea. Many ancient thinkers believed in a connection between musical rhythm and the rhythm of the mind. What Lozanov and others were able to do was isolate the kinds of music that brought about the coveted state of relaxed alertness characterized by the alpha brain wave patterns.

Unfortunately, many of you will be dismayed when told that it is classical music in general, baroque in particular, that is the only Western music that achieves this. Some ancient Indian and Japanese music is also especially good. Sorry, but rock, rap, hip hop, country, heavy metal — in fact, almost all popular forms of music — not only lack this quality, but actually interfere with learning. Some of the more sophisticated forms of Gregorian chants, jazz, and bluegrass have the beneficial traits, but not to a significant enough level to be recommended to aid studying.

What this means is that under no circumstances should you listen to any popular music immediately before studying, during studying, or within an hour afterward. It is like a drug that blocks learning. Do not kid yourself! Listening to your favorite pop music while studying does *not* help you study.

Most of the underlying rhythms of baroque music are at a pace of 60 beats per minute. Exposure to this kind of rhythm in the specific structure of a baroque piece has been scientifically proven to enhance the synchronization and activation of the various learning centers in the brain. The music also stimulates those alpha brain wave patterns that are so beneficial to superstudying.

BAROQUE MUSIC

But it is more than the rhythms of the music that creates this beneficial effect on the brain. The structure of a baroque musical piece is a reflection of an overall philosophy that was prevalent in arts, higher culture, and intellectual discourse during that period (c. 1650-1750). The thinkers and artists of the baroque era were striving for order and harmony with humankind's natural higher abilities. Art, buildings, literature, and music were supposed to be created to encourage harmony with nature, human nature, and the universe in general.

Composers formed their musical creations to stimulate this harmony. Many of them saw the interrelationship between music, philosophy, and mathematics and used combinations of these studies to enhance the scale, symmetry, and serenity of their music.

There is still an important place for the use of this kind of music in a more conventional learning environment. Simply using some baroque music in your study preparation can give you many of the benefits. It will aid in right/left brain integration, thus helping you to bring more of your seven intelligences into play.

Here is a list of musical selections you can use to make your own study prep concert. The effects are more pronounced with superior recordings, so try to listen to performances on Deutsche Grammophon or EMI Records. It makes a difference. You may also be able to find a compilation album containing a sampling of works by various composers.

- Johann Pachelbel — Canon in D Major
- Antonio Vivaldi — *The Four Seasons;* Concerto in D Major for guitar and strings
- Johann Sebastian Bach — Harpsicord Concerto in C Major; Orchestral Suite no. 3 in D Major
- Tomaso Albinoni — Adagio in G Minor
- Arcangelo Corelli — Concerto Grosso no. 10 in F Major; Concerto Grosso no. 8, opus 6 in G minor
- George Frideric Handel — *Water Music*

4. Activate your knowledge

Now that you are calm, relaxed, alert, and feeling good about yourself, there is one more step in preparation that will improve your study efficiency. Before you open your books to begin studying, you should "activate" your prior knowledge of the subject.

Even if you are at the beginning of a new course, the chances are very good that you already know something about the subject. The farther you go in the class, the more you will know. Your study sessions will always be more efficient if you warm up the part of your memory that has stored this knowledge. It doesn't matter if the knowledge is superficial, or even wrong. Because, as you will see in the next chapter, memory works by association, so the more active past associations you have, the more likely you are to remember something new.

You do not create new memories in isolation. They are attached to something that's already in there. For example, if you are taking a course in history and the topic is Napoleon Bonaparte, you already have many associations in your mind about him. You can't help it. If you take time and effort to quickly review what you already know about Napoleon before studying the material in your text, you will have hooks on which to hang new information. You will expand an already existing picture of his life and career. You will also correct errors in your knowledge banks (e.g., he wasn't a native Frenchman; he was Corsican).

How do you do this "activation"? It should not take a long time. Using a pencil and a piece of scrap paper, scribble down all the things you can remember about the topic and the key items you've learned so far. Do not edit yourself; just write everything that comes into your mind for two to five minutes. Then stop.

The goal is not to write an essay or come up with a complete list. Your purpose is like that of an athlete who stretches before serious training or competition. The athlete wants to get the blood circulating to the muscles and have them warmed up. You are warming up your mind.

e. Sequences for preparing yourself to study

Now that you know about these ideas for preparation, you should practice them consistently so that they become usable tools in your toolbox. They don't take a lot of time and are not very difficult, but it does take a conscious effort to master them. Your goal should be to develop these preparation techniques to a level that makes them instantly available whenever you want to employ them. You want to be able to construct a study preparation sequence from any of these techniques.

Once you have practiced these techniques and are used to doing a good preparation sequence, you can run through an entire checklist of things and be fully prepared for study in a fraction of the time it took you to read this chapter. Ideally, you should not need to spend more than ten minutes in this prestudy phase. But the results you earn for the time spent are incredible.

You want to achieve five basic things to put you in the best possible state of mind for studying. You want to —

(a) feel relaxed, not stressed or anxious,

(b) have an open, alert mind,

(c) breathe with maximum efficiency, getting a lot of oxygen to the brain,

(d) feel positive about your ability as a learner, and

(e) prime your brain for study by having activated prior knowledge.

If you're not prepared in any of these areas, you now have some tools to get you there. Remember, you are not limited to the suggestions in this chapter. You should develop your own techniques once you are comfortable with the basic principles.

Exercise #4 presents some sample preparation sequences. Experiment with them and find what works for you. It is wise to have a feel for what works best in a given situation. It all depends on how you feel at the time and what you are attempting to study.

f. A final word about preparation

This is one of the longest chapters in the book. It is that way for a reason. Preparation is probably the most important aspect of study technique. If you do the things recommended in this chapter, and don't change your study habits in any other way, you will see a dramatic improvement in your results. Without question, these preparatory techniques will have more positive impact on your grades and overall learning ability than anything else in this book or any other study skills book.

EXERCISE #4
PREPARATION SEQUENCES

Sequence 1

1. Sit comfortably in your study chair with feet flat on the floor and hands resting in your lap.

2. Perform a sequence of ten natural breaths without pauses (beginner pattern — see Exercise #1).

3. Close your eyes and visualize your sanctuary. Spend time in the whirlpool you installed in your living quarters (don't spend too long here or you'll get too groggy rather than nicely relaxed).

4. While in the whirlpool, recite three of your affirmations ten times each.

5. Open your eyes and do ten more natural breaths without pauses (beginner pattern).

6. Quickly write out (or recite out loud) the key points about the subject you will study first. What do you already know about it?

Sequence 2

1. Sit comfortably in your study chair with feet flat on the floor and hands resting in your lap.

2. Perform a sequence of ten natural breaths without pauses (beginner pattern — see Exercise #1).

3. Close your eyes and go through the muscle relaxation exercise.

4. Open your eyes and do ten natural breaths with pauses at a level comfortable for you (intermediate pattern).

5. Quickly write out (or recite out loud) the key points about the subject you will study first. What do you already know about it?

Sequence 3

1. Sit comfortably in your study chair with feet flat on the floor and hands resting in your lap.

2. Play a selection of baroque music while performing a sequence of ten natural breaths with or without pauses, depending on your level of proficiency (see Exercise #1). Keep the music going throughout this sequence.

3. Recite two of your affirmations five times each.

4. Close your eyes and visualize how you will feel when this exam is over. Picture yourself handing in the completed answer sheet. How will you feel at that moment? How will you feel before the exam starts, knowing you have prepared well? Imagine the sense of calm and confidence.

5. Open your eyes and do ten more natural breaths without pauses.

6. Quickly write out (or recite out loud) the key points about the subject you will study first. What do you already know about it?

5.

Memory

Learning is the process by which we create memories and the mechanisms for retrieving those memories when needed (either consciously or unconsciously). Memory is the key. Therefore, it's worth spending some time on a review of some of the basics of memory theory and how you can apply it to your studying.

When specific recommendations are provided in the chapters on time management, reading, note making, and exam preparation, they are based on the general theories of the brain and intelligence outlined in chapter 3 and on the specific realities of the way your memory works.

This chapter provides insights into why some study strategies work so much better than others and why you may have been working very hard but not achieving the results you'd hoped for — certainly not the results your effort deserved. This is where you begin to see the difference between working smarter and harder.

Here are the basics. You must take what is relevant for you based on the fundamentals.

a. Principles of memory

1. What is memory?

Put simply, memories are neural traces created in the brain. They are the linkages or connections between neurons that constitute the chemical bond caused by strong associations.

These chemical links are created by several different kinds of action, the most common being an initial sensory or emotional event, and sustained repetition of that event.

2. The three Rs of memory

It is helpful to think of memory as having three stages, each representing a different level of intensity: registration, retention, and recall.

REGISTRATION

The first stage, *registration,* is the stage at which something comes to your attention and has meaning for you. Whether or not you turn this initial registration into a permanent memory will depend on your purpose. If you simply want to remember a phone number long enough to dial it, then you won't go any further. If you want to remember the phone number of someone important to you, then you have to do something more to make it a permanent memory.

RETENTION

Retention is the stage at which you make a conscious decision to remember something, and you must decide on how to make that happen. Your goal is to retain the information for a long time.

RECALL

The third stage is *recall.* Retention is not much good without the ability to recall the information when it is needed. Therefore, the technique used to retain it must be one that will enhance the likelihood that you can access the information at some time in the future.

3. Basic memory model

The three Rs of memory can be understood in terms of this simple model. You have two kinds of memory: short-term and long-term.

Short-term memory is where things are stored at the registration stage of remembering. If you don't do something active with the item (e.g., write it down, draw a picture, or say it out loud) to make it a permanent memory, it will be forgotten. (See section **b.2.** below for a more detailed discussion of being active.) Your short-term memory has an average capacity of seven items, although it can range from as little as four to a maximum of ten.

Test this out for yourself. Make up a list of 4, 7, 10, and 15 items. Make each word completely unrelated to the others. Read each list only once, put it face down, then try to write out as many words as you can. You will find that you can easily remember the list of 4 immediately after seeing it. The list of 7 will be more difficult, and you may miss 1 or 2 items. The list of 10 will strain your capacity, and you will miss 3 or 4 items. From the list of 15, you will never remember more than 10 and will likely average 7 or 8 at best, no matter how many times you try it.

If you make a deliberate effort through rehearsal and review, you can transfer information into your long-term memory. The more often you review that information after it is stored there, the greater your chances of avoiding memory decay and being able to recall it easily and quickly (see Figure #1).

FIGURE #1
SHORT-TERM
MEMORY
TRANSFER

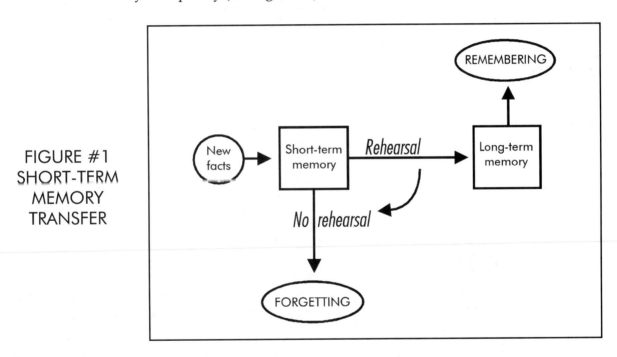

4. Forgetting

The importance of beginning the review/rehearsal process as soon as possible after something enters your short-term memory is graphically illustrated by the Ebbinghaus Curve (named for 19th-century German memory researcher Hermann Ebbinghaus).

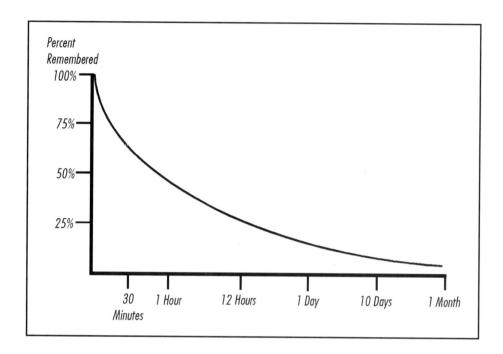

FIGURE #2
EBBINGHAUS
CURVE

As you can see from Figure #2, if you don't actively do something to create long-term memories, you will very quickly forget most of what you encounter. This has important implications for most students. It's a lazy, bad habit to passively read textbooks or just sit and listen to lectures. You will usually rationalize that you are concentrating on what you are reading or what is being said and that you will make notes later or reread the important passages.

Don't kid yourself. If you are not active with the material while you are first encountering it, and then delay active remembering activities, you will forget it!

5. Multi-sensory effect

The more senses you employ in the rehearsal and review stages, the more you will remember (see Figure #3). Use these in conjunction with your many intelligences, and give yourself a far better chance of embedding material in your long-term memory.

FIGURE #3
REMEMBERING
GRAPH

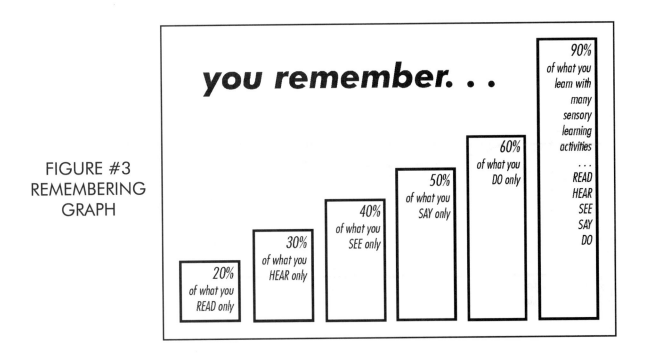

6. Recency and primacy effects

Go back to the list of 15 items you created. When you tested yourself, chances are that most of the items you remembered were either near the beginning of the list or near the end. Dozens of studies have proven the existence of the "recency effect" and the "primacy effect." The latter means that you tend to have better recall for things that happen at the beginning of an event or situation. The former means that you tend to remember things that happened most recently (see Figure #4).

What does this mean for your studying? If you remember more of what you study at the beginning and the end of a study session, doesn't it make sense to have a lot of beginnings and endings in your study schedule? (See Figure #5.)

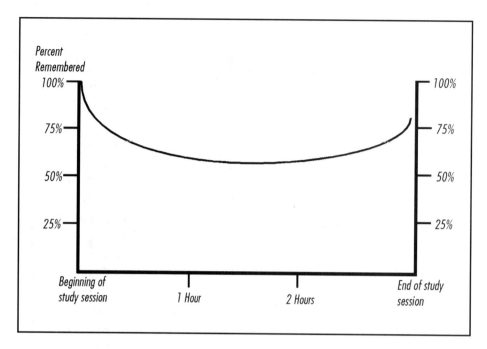

FIGURE #4
REMEMBERING
CURVE A

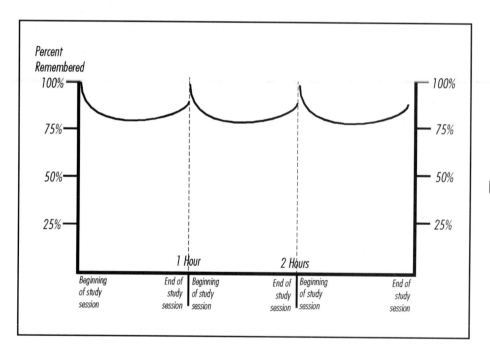

FIGURE #5
REMEMBERING
CURVE B

64

7. Similarity effect

It is easier to remember a variety of things if you group them together. By grouping, you will be able to recall much more information than you would normally be able to.

Try it for yourself. Here is a list of 20 words. Look quickly at each once, then cover up the list and see how many you can remember. According to the basic model of memory, you should only be able to remember 10.

If, however, you knew in advance that each word would come under one of five categories, you would probably be able to recall the entire list.

| 1. Rose |
| 2. Car |
| 3. Pen |
| 4. Desk |
| 5. Light bulb |
| 6. Airplane |
| 7. Bed |
| 8. Truck |
| 9. Crayon |
| 10. Firefly |
| 11. Daffodil |
| 12. Star |
| 13. Table |
| 14. Chalk |
| 15. Train |
| 16. Iris |
| 17. Matches |
| 18. Pencil |
| 19. Tulip |
| 20. Chair |

Flowers	Vehicles	Furniture	Things that emit light	Things that write
Rose	Car	Desk	Light bulb	Pen
Iris	Truck	Chair	Star	Pencil
Tulip	Train	Table	Matches	Chalk
Daffodil	Airplane	Bed	Firefly	Crayon

See how simple it is? Once you organize the list, you need to remember only five categories and only four items in each category. Each is within the comfort level of seven for your short-term memory and well below the uncomfortable maximum.

This is a simplified example, but you see how the principle of organization, or "clustering," can help improve the capacity of your memory. The same basic theory can have a dramatic effect on how much you will remember for a test.

8. Association effect

The example above works so well because your memory works best when it makes associations. Linking things that are similar is one form of this associative pattern that enhances memory. It works because you are linking things you want to remember with what is already in your brain.

There are other, more powerful, kinds of associative relationships you will want to activate as you improve your memory power.

(a) Sensory

Music, when soft voices die,

Vibrates in memory;

Odors, when sweet violets
   sicken,

Live within the sense they
   quicken

   Percy Bysshe Shelley

Using many different sensory associations improves your memory. The most important is visual. Research proves that your memory is essentially a visual mechanism, and, therefore, it makes sense to concentrate on developing your visual associations.

This does not mean you have to have a crystal clear mental picture of everything you're trying to remember. Most people, even those with good visualization skills, do not have vivid, photographic-type pictures in their heads. But the visual connections do get stronger the longer you practice.

If you don't believe that your memory is mostly visual, try this exercise. Try to remember where everything is in your bedroom or kitchen. Where do you keep your socks? Where are the coffee cups? How many windows are in the room? Is the kitchen table on the left or the right as you come in the door?

How do you remember all that? It isn't from a list. It isn't from smell or musical association. It's visual. Perhaps it isn't in technicolor, but you are working from a mental picture.

Other senses are strongly tied to memory, especially smell and sound. But visual associations are the strongest of all.

How vast a memory has

love.

   Alexander Pope

(b) Emotional

Things to which you have a strong emotional association are also more easily remembered: the pride you felt when you won an award, the pain when someone you cared about died, the thrill of the first kiss with someone you love. These are strong memories because of the intensity of the emotions attached to them.

(c) Intensity

The factor that makes sensory and emotional associations work so well as memory evocators is their intensity. The more intense the feeling, color, smell, pain, or joy, the more likely you are never to forget it. It creates a strong chemical bond in your brain very quickly and its uniqueness makes it easy to recall.

(d) Meaning

After senses and feelings, the most effective way to create associations is with meaning. It is easy to remember something if it has meaning for you. Obviously, the more personal associations of vision and emotion are better, but if those aren't appropriate, find meaning in the use of language.

If you can make an acronym or a sentence out of a list of words you need to remember, it will take on more meaning. It's easier to remember the acronym S.C.U.B.A. than the full description of self-contained underwater breathing apparatus. You can remember the planets of our solar system in their order from the sun if you can recall this sentence: My very elegant master just served up nine pineapples. The first letter in each word is the first letter in the name of a planet, in order from the sun.

It's easy to remember a sentence because our brain is trained to store and recall the patterns of language.

9. Weirdness effect

A version of the intensity factor in associations is the "weirdness" effect. You are more likely to remember things that are unusual, outrageous, or out of place.

Go back to the list of 20 words in subsection **7**. If words such as Zulu or Zoroastrian or Ninja are added to the list, you will be able to remember them even though they do not fit into any category. The reason is that the words are very different. They stand out and that makes them memorable. Adding a "weirdness" element to the things you are trying to memorize will increase the limits of your memory.

Oh better than the mining

Of a gold-crowned king

Is the safe-kept memory

Of a lovely thing.

Sara Teasdale

My	Mercury
Very	Venus
Elegant	Earth
Master	Mars
Just	Jupiter
Served	Saturn
Up	Uranus
Nine	Neptune
Pineapples	Pluto

10. Specificity effect

The specific, unequivocal, or definite are more easily stored and recalled than that which tends to elude easy definition or finality. For example, it is easier to learn dates and names of prime ministers than it is to remember the theory of historicism and apply it to the study of the Middle Ages as practiced in Victorian Britain.

11. Repetition effect

Of course, the more you repeat what you want to embed in long-term memory, the better you will remember it. Associations, recency, weirdness, specificity, and activity mean nothing if you do not drill yourself in the things you want to remember.

b. Improving your memory for studying

Your memory is already pretty good. Most people focus on the deficiencies of their memory because they are unaware of it until they have forgotten something important at precisely the worst time. If you forget a doctor's appointment or your mom's birthday, chances are you will blame your supposedly inadequate memory.

The fact that your memory is good enough to remember tens of thousands of words and their proper use as a language rarely registers with people as a prodigious memory feat. It is. If you tried to make a list of everything you already have stored in your memory, it would take longer than the rest of your life. And that's only the stuff you are able to recall. That's the good news.

The bad news is that your basic memory is so good at quietly storing and recalling enough to let you function in society that you probably don't make any effort to improve it. Things are fine at the current comfort level even though you are using a small fraction of your memory's capacity.

There is nothing wrong with your memory that a little exercise wouldn't cure. As a student trying to learn material for examination or retention for a job function, you need to make the effort to push yourself out of that comfort zone. Here are some of the simple things you can do.

1. Relax

Remember from chapter 3 that the higher brain functions are more efficient when you are relaxed and free from stress. No matter how many of the techniques and memory tricks you use from this list, you can't make effective use of your memory if you grit your teeth and try to shove the material into your mind by sheer determination.

Relax. Enjoy the learning and remembering. If external factors have you tense and feeling stressed, use some of the relaxation techniques in chapter 4 to properly prepare yourself.

2. Be active

Being active is the key to all effective studying. Passively looking at the words on the page is what most people do and never get beyond. You must be active.

Read out loud. Teach the material to someone. Make up a rhyme. Rewrite the key ideas in your own words. Draw a picture. Review the material silently. (Beware: "silent" does not mean you can be passive. For instance, you are being active when you mentally connect the material to something you already know, or test your recall of a list of things by reviewing it backward without looking.)

All these activities require your mind to work with the material, reorganize it, and, in the process, make it part of you. As long as you are a passive studier, the information will always be somebody else's.

Great works are performed, not by strength, but perseverance.

Samuel Johnson

3. Use many intelligences

The brain has seven essential intelligences. Most people actively use only one or two in study situations. This will obviously severely limit your memory. As you develop your repertoire of study and memory techniques, make sure you incorporate as many of your intelligences as possible.

Making a rhyme uses your linguistic as well as musical intelligence. Drawing a picture (especially a mind map — see chapter 12) uses the visual/spatial intelligence. Teaching someone uses interpersonal as well as linguistic memory — even physical memory if you use a lot of movement and hand gestures in your teaching. Rewriting in your own words uses logical, linguistic, and physical memory. (The act of writing is inherently physical and activates that part of the brain.)

4. Use smaller chunks of time on many different tasks

Organize your study sessions to take advantage of the primacy and recency effects. Since your ability to retain information is at its peak at the beginning and at the end of a study session, doesn't it make sense to create as many beginnings and endings as possible?

For example, if you have two hours available to do your studying, the most inefficient way to spend the time is to use it all on one task in one subject without a break. Studies have shown that 30 to 45 minutes is the maximum amount of time you can spend on a concentrated study task before you start to experience a degradation in your ability to retain what you are learning. Therefore, you should divide your two-hour block into four sessions of 30 minutes each. This approach gives you enough time to do something reasonably significant, but is short enough to prevent the deep "forgetting" trough you see in Figure #4. You also increase the number of those highly productive beginnings and endings from two to eight.

There is also a great advantage to be gained if you vary the activity in each 30-minute block. Study a different subject and do a different activity in each study block. For instance, read psychology in the first session, do math problems next, then practice Japanese vocabulary out loud, and finish by study reading history (chapter 10 discusses study reading in detail).

By engaging a different intelligence each time on a different subject, your brain actually consolidates and reviews the previous session in the "background" while it focuses a different part on the new task. You will learn more, faster, with a lot less pain and boredom than by spending two hours on the same subject.

5. Chunk material

When studying and reviewing, try to organize the material so common elements are reviewed together. Remember that it is easier to memorize five headings with five items each than to try and cram 25 seemingly unrelated pieces of data into your long-term memory. Use this technique whenever you have lists of items you need to remember. There won't always be a pattern, but the mere act of analyzing the list in search of patterns will aid your memorization.

6. Create strong associations

Take the extra few seconds it requires to make strong **sensory** and emotional associations in your mind. You remember what has meaning, so, whenever possible, try to imbue the information with meaning that is personal to you.

This is probably a new concept for most students, so be prepared to do some experimentation with it. The easiest kinds of associations when you are beginning are emotional ones and those that are strongly visual. The best way of using your mind's strong affinity for visual association to help studying and learning is to use Tony Buzan's concept of mind maps, the basics of which are discussed in chapter 12. Once you try Buzan's method on your homework, you will be astounded by how easy it is and how profoundly it will **affect** your memory.

A thousand fantasies begin to throng into my memory.

John Milton

7. Practice output

Practicing output is essential for the recall stage of memory. Don't get stuck in repetitious rehearsal that focuses only on getting the material INTO long-term memory. Practice getting it out — under pressure. Practice using the actual kind of exam questions you will be required to answer. Make up your own multiple-choice or essay questions and practice answering them.

8. Review early and regularly

You can make dramatic improvements in the amount of information you retain and recall simply by doing a short review of the material on a regular basis. For example, you can increase your memory of a three-hour lecture by up to 500% simply by using three-minute review sessions. Review the material immediately after the lecture, then repeat the review after one hour, one day, one week, one month, two months, etc. This easy technique will change the normal "forgetting curve" shown in Figure #2. With review, your curve will change and look like Figure #6.

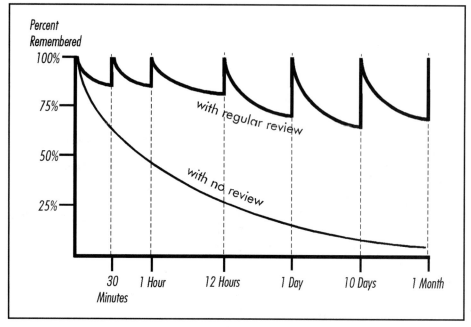

Percent Remembered

100%

75%

with regular review

50%

with no review

25%

30 Minutes   1 Hour   12 Hours   1 Day   10 Days   1 Month

FIGURE #6
THE IMPACT OF
REVIEW

9. Develop basic memory aids

Using what you have learned in this book, develop your own toolbox of techniques to aid your memory and help increase its capability:

- Make flash cards.
- Make mind maps (see chapter 12).
- Create mnemonic devices (see subsection **a. 8.(d)** above).
- Make rhymes, rhythms, and songs.

10. Practice, practice, practice

Make a conscious effort to practice your memory skills. Nothing will change if you do not consistently practice new skills and techniques. There won't be any overnight miracle to motivate you, but improvement will happen faster than you think.

Don't try to do it all at once. Remember that the human organism resists change to its current status, even if the change is a good one. Introduce new approaches gradually, and give them two to three months to have an effect.

No practice means you are wasting your incredible memory potential.

Fond memory brings the light.

Thomas Moore

11. Sleep on it

Research shows that sleep is a necessary component to good memory. Aside from the obvious need for enough sleep to remain healthy and mentally alert, the brain actually uses the sleep period to consolidate things in the long-term memory. What you review immediately before going to sleep is what your brain will most quickly and efficiently file away. It's almost as if your brain needs some "down time" to process the associations and connections required to make long-term memories.

Test this on yourself. You will find that you remember things much more easily and effectively if you review just before sleep and then test yourself in the morning. You will remember more this way than if you study the material in the morning and test yourself that same evening without any intervening sleep. You are making use of the consolidation effects of the delta brain waves discussed in chapter 3.

12. Explore advanced memory aids

Once you have experienced the amazing improvements produced by just a little consistent practice of these basic ideas, you may want to try some intermediate and advanced memory improvement techniques. There are several well-known systems you can learn that will have a huge impact on your study memory. Some examples are —

- the Memory Peg System,
- the Linking System,
- the Location Method
  (also called the Roman Room System), and
- the Rhyming Method.

If you are interested in developing some of these systems, you should do some research to determine which, if any, are suitable for your learning style and learning needs. The best survey of such methods is Tony Buzan's *Use Your Perfect Memory*, (3rd edition, Penguin Books).

One must have a good memory to be able to keep the promises one makes.

Friedrich Nietzsche

6.

Concentration

a. What is concentration?

Studying requires long periods of sustained focus on new knowledge and working with that knowledge so it becomes a permanent part of long-term memory. This demands "concentration" — the ability to work intensely at a task to the exclusion of every other demand on your attention.

For many students, this is the most difficult part of becoming a good student. They lack the capacity to concentrate for more than a few minutes before something else claims their attention and the mind wanders from the task at hand.

Much has been made in the popular media about the diminishing attention span of younger generations. TV and video games are supposed to have had a detrimental effect on the ability to concentrate for the sustained periods required to learn. Is this popular conception true? YES!

TV and Nintendo are major culprits. They rob us of the capability to focus on one thing long enough to delve into it in depth. The quick cuts of music videos and the short periods of program between commercials are valid villains. But it is more than that. Life is more complex and there are more things competing for our attention. So much choice in how to spend our time means that most people skip along the surface of many things without exploring the depths of anything.

Is this a permanent condition? NO! Is there something that can be done to stop the rot and maybe even improve our ability to concentrate. YES! And, probably much to your surprise, it's relatively simple; not easy, but certainly simple.

The first step is to understand the three basic elements that get in the way of good concentration. Once you are aware of the nature of the problem, some of the strategies for solving it become obvious.

b. What interferes with concentration?

Lack of concentration means victory by the many different distractions. Distractions come in three forms: those from the outside environment, those from inside you, and those that are a result of not having a clear idea of what you are supposed to be doing.

1. External distractions

Factors in your physical environment such as noise, lighting, air quality, and visual surroundings can all become serious distractions. Here are the main culprits:

- Uncomfortable chair
- Study surface that is too high or too low
- Street noise
- Music
- Poor light (too dim or too bright)
    - Too hot or too cold
    - Reminders of others things you need to do or would rather do (e.g., letters to write or magazines to read)
    - TV
    - Conversations from people at nearby tables
    - Friends interrupting you

Do you know anyone who has a problem with one or more of these concentration robbers? Perhaps you know that someone very, very well?

2. Internal distractions

Distractions that originate from inside you are more insidious. Even in a quiet, comfortable, well-lit study place, the most significant enemies to your concentration will be able to find you. Sometimes they have physical origins:

- Lack of sleep
- Poor diet
- Lack of exercise
- Illness
- Physical injury

More often the internal distractions are stress related and have emotional origins (some major, some minor):

- Relationship problems
- Friction with family or friends
- Worry about money
- Anxiety about other courses and the work needed for them

3. Lack of focus or goals

Sometimes it's hard to concentrate because you do not have a clear, firm answer to the nagging question: "What am I doing this to myself for?" You would rather be doing other things such as watching TV, or hanging out with your friends, or playing floor hockey, or reading a magazine, or just about anything but your calculus homework.

Occasionally this can be a sign that you are not taking the right courses. But, more often than not, it's a symptom of having no clear goals. If you can't see a valuable connection between the task at hand and a short-term goal, which is connected to an intermediate goal, which is connected to a long-term life goal, then it's easy to say "the hell with this" and let yourself be distracted by some meaningless diversion like your computer game.

c. How can you improve your concentration?

It's impossible to eliminate all the distractions that will interfere with your concentration. There are, however, many factors you can control. Make up your mind to control that which is in your power to control, and to ignore (at least for the length of your study session) that which is beyond your influence.

Is not life a thousand times too short for us to bore ourselves?

Friedrich Nietzsche

Get rid of the TV and other electronic time-thieves. This sounds harsh and unrealistic, but for some people there is no other way to say it. Many students are addicted to TV and video games; TV and video games have gone beyond harmless entertainment and become thieves of their time and their ability to concentrate. Wean yourself away from TV and video games until they are out of your life completely when there is studying to be done.

Prepare. The preparation of your study environment and your mind are the easiest and most immediately effective concentration helpers available. (See chapter 4.)

Follow the guidelines for setting up a proper study place. Take the time to get yourself into the proper state of mind to ease stress and anxiety before you open your books. If you skipped reading chapter 4, go back to it now. It will solve 80% of your problems with distractions.

Take care of yourself. Make certain you do all you can to give yourself the physical capacity for the mental workout good studying requires.

- Get plenty of **sleep**. This is often the first casualty of a heavy study schedule, but it's a mistake to sacrifice your sleep. The time you do spend on your studies will be 30% to 70% wasted if you are not well rested.

- **Diet** is important. Eat as much fruit and vegetables as you can. Avoid excesses of fat and sugar — especially just before you study.

- Get some **exercise**. Your mind works more effectively when your body is in tune. If you are not athletically inclined, make sure you walk each day.

- Try to lead a **balanced life**. Have fun! It's easier to concentrate on your work if you are not giving up the rest of your life.

Make concrete goals. The importance of setting goals is discussed in chapter 8. They are essential when you have to answer the question about why you are doing this to yourself. It is also very important that you develop the skills required to set proper individual study goals.

Having specific, reasonable, achievable, concrete, relevant goals each time you sit down to do homework will be the best concentration builder you can have. Nothing keeps you more focused on a task than being certain what that task is . . . and knowing when it will be over.

Make lists. Make use of the power of lists. If the strain of trying to remember day-to-day things is intruding on your study concentration, chances are it's because you haven't done the one simple thing to make sure you won't forget.

Write it down.

It's amazing the number of people who add to the stress of our complex society and their busy, busy lives by trying to keep all the details in their memory. Get into the habit of writing down all the mundane but essential things such as your grandparents' anniversary or your nephew's birthday; it will keep the information from popping into your head just when you are trying to understand the intricacies of organic chemistry.

Keep a stress file or worry list. If there is something beyond the mundane that is causing you anxiety, you may need a special kind of list. Issues like personal problems and money difficulties can certainly interfere with your study concentration. When these cause your mind to wander and worry, try writing them down on a special list.

The symbolism of writing a problem down and setting the paper aside or putting it in a file folder does give you surprising temporary relief. Obviously it will not solve the problem, but it can often remove it from your consciousness long enough for you to return to learning. The problem will still be there in its original condition when you finish studying, so why let it prevent you from getting your work done?

Make a plan to fight back. All the strategies are fine and will help you minimize distractions. But what you're doing is preventing things from depleting your existing powers of concentration. They don't do much

to actually increase your concentration levels. If that is a problem for you, then you also need to make a conscious decision to improve that part of your mental toolbox.

It can be done. The next section shows you one simple technique that will actually increase the length of time you can study with superior concentration.

d. A concentration fitness plan for studying

The principle behind this proven technique is similar to that used by weekend joggers who want to become marathon runners. You will gradually increase the amount of time you work at your studies with good concentration.

It's unrealistic to expect that you will go from one minute of concentration to a full half hour all at once. You must build up your study "endurance" slowly. However, it doesn't take long to experience amazing results. If you follow just this simple technique you can triple, even quadruple, your concentration endurance in just two weeks.

Step 1   Have at least two study tasks prepared in advance, preferably three tasks.

Step 2   Begin to study as usual.

Step 3   The instant you realize your mind is wandering or you are worrying about personal things that are distracting you, STOP TRYING TO STUDY.

Step 4   If the distraction is something that you should put on your reminder list or worry list, do so immediately.

Step 5   Decide to move on to one of the other study tasks. BUT before you do . . .

Step 6   Do one more small, easy item of work from the current task. For example, if it's math, do one more problem. If it's history, read one more page. If it's Spanish, memorize one more new word. Really focus yourself and use every ounce of your concentration powers for this brief time.

Even if you seem to be back in the flow of the first study task, you must stop after the one extra item. Close those books, put them away, and move on to the next task. **Step 7**

Repeat the process starting with Step 2. **Step 8**

The purpose of this simple process is to push yourself past what you are normally used to doing, but not too far. If you stop after feeling the success of doing one more thing, you accomplish many positive things that will soon start to have a cumulative, cascading effect on your concentration.

First, you see how easy it is to refocus yourself after momentarily losing your concentration. Having your mind wander is natural. What you must learn is how to keep the occurrences to a minimum and how to return your attention to task as soon as possible.

Second, you end your session with that subject on a positive note. You probably feel that you could continue on as you've got a "second wind." That's a good time to stop. Concentration will increase as you build up a lot of positive experiences you've had with concentration. If you always push yourself to the point of failure and have nothing left, the dispiriting feelings will also accumulate. The positive ending from one session will be the first thing in your mind the next time you open that textbook, which will, in turn, enhance your concentration at the beginning of the new session.

Finally, a series of "just one more" study items also begins to accumulate. These will be learned very efficiently and recalled easily. It's amazing how quickly the feeling of learning with high concentration becomes something you want to repeat as often as possible. Just try this technique for a month and enjoy the wonderful effect it will have on your concentration.

e. What to do if nothing is working

How do you study efficiently when nothing seems to help you concentrate for long periods? Some days, no matter how hard you try to concentrate, it just isn't there. How do you make good use of the time anyway?

First we form habits,

then they form us.

Conquer your bad

habits, or they'll

conquer you.

Dr. Robert Gilbert

- Don't get down on yourself. If you make an honest effort, and have been actively working to improve your overall concentration ability, give yourself a break this time. Accept that today is an off day.
- Use something else from your toolbox that will still make your study time productive.
- Practice with your flash cards (discussed in chapter 9).
- Preview your textbook chapters instead of "study reading" (discussed in chapter 10).
- Review lecture notes (discussed in chapter 11).
- Draw a new mind map (discussed in chapter 12).
- Make new flash cards (discussed in chapter 9).
- Take a break, relax (take a trip to your sanctuary), and try again in a few minutes.

7.

The 12 principles of study skills

(A summary of the story so far)

It's time to review the essence of what has been discussed so far and preview what underlies the chapters to come. Building on the foundation of what we know about brain physiology and memory theory, here are some principles that guide the rest of the topics.

You should read the preceding chapters at least twice to make sure the important points sink in. They really do give you an inspiring introduction to the astounding power of your brain and how to prepare yourself to use it effectively. If you're not convinced, read the summary provided in the following principles.

a. Principle 1: Believe in yourself

Your brain is the most complex piece of bioengineering in the known universe. Every brain has genius capacity — even yours. It takes time, effort, and guided study to get access to this potential, but it is possible for anyone to do if he or she wants to badly enough.

Set goals for yourself and develop plans for achieving them. See chapter 8 for details about working on this underutilized set of skills.

To successfully travel that long road to your goals, you must believe in yourself. In chapter 4 you learned about surrounding yourself with positive messages and reminders of past success. Remember that you are a confident and capable learner. You can learn anything. You have genius potential and every technique from this book that you use will help you fulfill that possibility.

b. Principle 2: Prepare

The difference between mediocre performance and excellent grades can often be the quality of your preparation. Preparing your study environment, your attitude, and your focus will have an amazingly positive impact on the effectiveness of your learning activity.

Most people don't plan to fail; they just fail to plan!

Anonymous

The basics in chapter 4 are for studying at home, before class, in preparation for an exam, before an oral presentation — every time! This is not silly busywork. These are valid, important study steps most people neglect. Smart students don't neglect them.

c. Principle 3: Organize yourself and your work

Organize yourself and organize your work. Always have a plan for your studying. Write out that plan. Review your plan constantly, and revise it constantly.

It is that simple. The difficult part is coming up with a plan that works. It's difficult because it rarely comes out right the first time.

Most people fail at this because they give up when the first attempt at planning does not work out perfectly. The best thing to do is to expect changes and be ready for the process. Needing to make changes in your plan does not mean failure — it means inexperience at planning and life being inevitably inconsiderate with our plans. Quitting all planning when things go off the rails — THAT really is failure.

Use the principles in this chapter and throughout the book to guide you, and your planning will be more effective. Planning is a kind of mental muscle: it will improve the more often you use it.

d. Principle 4: Spend time on what matters

Set priorities and make sure you are spending time on tasks that will help you accomplish the goals that are those priorities. The manner in which you get there is the essence of planning. If your goal is to pass your real estate exam or graduate from high school or earn your degree, then you have a lot of work to do.

In the midst of writing down plans, developing self-discipline, and making schedules, many students begin to feel that school is consuming their life. That is missing the point.

The work will be there anyway. You cannot avoid it. Studying and homework are a major part of what it means to be a student and a learner. You can become a more effective learner using the information in this book, but there will still be work. But you can choose where the control in this situation will reside. Will you control the work or will the work have control over your life?

The work can control you if you neglect proper planning and study techniques until a crisis or a series of crises overwhelm you. If you let assignments and exam preparation pile up until the middle of the year, you will lose control of your life for the rest of the year. With so little time left before each due date or exam on your schedule, you no longer have much, if any, flexibility about when to take a break, spend time with friends, or just relax. You will be engaged in damage control — a situation that is very stressful and never leads to optimum academic performance or good grades.

e. Principle 5: Discipline yourself

There is no substitute for self-control and discipline. The best study techniques, tricks, and hints are useless if you have no willpower to put them into practice. It helps your discipline if you have goals, an organized plan of action, and a strong belief in yourself, but you must also have the desire to keep at it when the going isn't easy. This is how the study techniques become second nature, and that's when your abilities really begin to take off.

Discipline in pursuit of your goals and dreams is not a restriction of your freedom. Those things that distract you from dreams are the real limitations. If one of your goals is to gain access to the genius potential inside you, to become the

In the last analysis, our only freedom is the freedom to discipline ourselves.

Bernard Baruch

confident superlearner you've always wanted to be, then any discipline it takes to stay on that path is freeing, not constricting.

f. Principle 6: Be persistent

Keepa going!

Masaaki Hatsumi
34th Grandmaster,
Togakure-ryu Ninjutsu

Just keep on keeping on. Persistence is more important than talent, genius, or luck. All those will be useless without persistence, but persistence can bring success without them.

g. Principle 7: Divide and conquer

The concept of "divide and conquer" is central to successfully completing any large study task such as a term paper, preparing for final examinations, or reading a thick textbook. Understanding how it works will have a wonderful effect on your procrastination problems. (The chapters dealing with memory and time management will give you more details.)

Simply, you analyze the task, divide it into smaller separate tasks, and make a written list of all the smaller tasks. The final step is to put the tasks in order of priority.

The drops of rain make a hole in the stone not by violence, but by oft falling.

Lucretius

Start with the first small step, complete it, cross it off the list, and go on to the next step. This process makes it easier to get started and to keep going. A short list with one big item on it that can't be crossed off until the whole thing is done can be discouraging. A long list that shrinks visibly is a good motivator. See chapter 8 for more details about the secrets of goal setting and motivation in your studying.

h. Principle 8: Become an information filter

The skill of filtering information is particularly valuable for college and university students. To survive and thrive in the midst of a university course load that can be overwhelming, you must become an information filter. It is not unusual for new students to panic when they first encounter the enormous amount of material to be read. When you practice good reading and note-making techniques, you are becoming an information filter; you are learning to distinguish between what is important to remember and what is not.

It takes practice to be able to filter out the unnecessary material. It takes even more practice to be confident that you have focused on the correct material. This is an area where

Principles 5 and 6 come into play. If you have the persistence to keep at it and the discipline to keep using proper study techniques, you will find yourself developing into an efficient filter.

i. Principle 9: Practice output as well as input

To practice output as well as input, it is helpful to think of the brain as a computer. The information you study is data input, the material is processed by the brain, and you are required to create output in the form of lab reports, essays, and exam answers. Unfortunately, our biological computers create output of varying levels of quality. It is not processed in the uniform, easily recallable units that get stored in a silicon chip.

To get the most out of the data, you must actively turn it into information that is useful. You must process it properly and PRACTICE OUTPUT. The latter is vital! Output is not automatic. You must devise several patterns of output so information is more easily recalled at a stressful moment, such as the middle of a final examination.

Chapter 3 discusses the various intelligences and this knowledge can give you an infinite stream of ideas for practicing output. The summary in chapter 5 of how memory works will give you more details about why repetition and output practice are so important.

We may be personally defeated, but our principles never.

William Lloyd Garrison

j. Principle 10: Do not fear mistakes

Mistakes are the best teachers. Don't be afraid to try something new just because you don't think you will get it right the first time. Without mistakes we would not have any information about how to do better the next time. Doing something wrong the first time simply tells you that you are outside your comfort zone and engaged in something new. Each time you do something new and outside your normal experience, your neurons are making more connections. Each time you identify a mistake, you've learned something about your task, and your brain remembers.

There are four steps to learning:

(a) Take an action and make mistakes.

(b) Review the result and identify mistakes.

(c) Decide how to do better the next time.

The higher up you go, the more mistakes you're allowed. Right at the top, if you make enough of them, it's considered to be your style.

Fred Astaire

(d) Go to the first step (which is now the "next time") and make different mistakes.

The only really disastrous mistake you can make is quitting after the first step. Mistakes help you eliminate wrong ways and guide you to the right way. With fewer mistakes you also have fewer chances of finding the right way to new skills, ideas, and feelings.

k. Principle 11: Use all your intelligences to create study tools

As chapter 3 makes clear, traditional school and study habits use only two of your seven major intelligences. As you develop your own toolbox of study skills, make a conscious effort to develop tools that make use of as many different intelligences as possible. Combine as many as you can as often as you can.

One should guide his

life by true principles.

Lucretius

Chapter 12 gives some examples of how to do this. Once you understand the ideas behind these, your own imagination will come up with dozens, even hundreds, more. The only limit on how many study tools are in your toolbox is the time you spend creating them. It is up to you.

l. Principle 12: Be active

All the best human data processing and output practice using many of your intelligences have one thing in common. They require that you be *active* with the material. You cannot be a passive reader or listener and expect to get much out of textbooks or lectures. It just won't happen.

All study, reading, and listening skills come down to the same thing: as soon as you hear or read something, you need to *do* something with it *immediately* in your brain. Think about it, evaluate it, and decide where it fits in relation to other information. Make it your own; make it part of you. This does not need to be time consuming; believe it or not, something significant can happen with just a few extra seconds of focus. But it does take a conscious effort.

Once you've done the extra thinking, you need to do a second active thing: write it down.

As you will see in chapters 11 and 12, this writing can take several forms and need not necessarily be traditional linear notes. Mind maps, pictures, doodles, and nonlinear words, for example, are all great ways to reinforce the learning by writing.

By engaging the material as soon as you encounter it and writing down the result, you are learning as you go. It is actually more efficient. Other activities such as taking verbatim lecture notes or highlighting large passages when reading usually just postpone learning. Why not do some learning the first time? Students who make an effort to be active are much more efficient because they waste less time.

This principle of being active rather than passive extends to all aspects of studying, especially preparing for exams. Being active is the only way you can properly process information and practice output.

Important principles may and must be inflexible.

Abraham Lincoln

Part III

The toolbox

8.

Goal setting and motivation

> Don't be afraid to take big steps. You can't cross a chasm in two small jumps.
>
> **David Lloyd George**

a. Why is goal setting important?

One of the key elements in study problems such as procrastination, poor concentration, and lack of motivation is lack of clear goals. Goal setting is a skill that needs development; it is a muscle that requires exercise. Without goals that are clearly defined, articulated, and written down, you will drift through life and certainly drift through your learning and study sessions.

If you do not have a clear vision of what is important to you in your life, you will follow the natural human tendency to be distracted by whatever crosses your path. It's not a bad thing to be curious and interested in those things that stray into your attention range. But without goals and priorities to get you back on track, you can easily dissipate your whole life on distractions.

There's a lot more to the art and skill of goal setting and creating action plans than getting yourself to follow through and take action. There are whole books devoted to this topic. This chapter touches just the surface. But at the immediate level of using goal setting to motivate your studying and keep you focused in each study session, you will soon have the beginning concepts.

b. Goal setting basics

Goal setting is a very important life skill and it will have a profound effect on your ability to concentrate and avoid procrastination, but it doesn't need to be complicated. Follow these basic guidelines and the process of goal setting will be inspiring, useful, and fun.

1. Start now

Why waste any more time? If your life has been drifting or you have difficulty getting down to your studies, you need to begin the habit of goal setting right now!

If it has been some time since you tried this kind of exercise, do it now. If your goals haven't been the motivators you hoped they would be, you have probably been ignoring the principles of including actions and expecting failure (see sections **7.** and **8.** below). Start over now.

2. Write down your goals

Always write your goals down. Keep a journal for long-term, intermediate, and short-term goals. Use to-do lists to keep track of the immediate goals that are part of your everyday life.

The principle behind writing down your goals is the same as the one behind making notes rather than relying on your memory. Not only does it make the goal more concrete, but the physical act of writing and expressing the idea in words engages at least two of your intelligences. If you try goal setting and making action plans using mind maps (see chapter 12), you add more intelligences to the mix.

Writing down your goals makes it easier to review them and remind yourself of priorities. Things become more of a commitment when they are written down.

3. Keep several lists according to time scale

Divide your goals into categories according to how distant they are in the future. Typical divisions are —

- long-term (five to ten years),
- intermediate-term (three to five years),
- short-term (one to two years), and
- immediate (this month, this week, or today).

4. Set priorities

You cannot do everything you want to do. You must set priorities or you will end up dissipating your energy and not accomplishing anything to your fullest potential. If you don't make choices for yourself, the inevitable drift that comes from too many goals will make choices for you — usually with mediocre results.

5. Challenge yourself

Keep your goals high enough to inspire you and reasonable enough to seem always within your reach. If your long-term goal is to be a lawyer, your intermediate goal must be to get accepted into law school. While you're at it, why not set your sights on getting into the best law school. If your long-term goal is to be a writer, why not plan to be a best-selling author rather than just barely making a living with your pen.

Excellence is never achieved by luck or accident. It requires that you push yourself beyond your comfort zone and challenge yourself. You still have to be reasonable, but there are always ways to achieve some version of your dreams. If you are 70 years old and have a fascination with the stars, it's probably unrealistic to set your goal to be an astronaut, but it would be possible to become an astronomer — a big challenge, but certainly within your reach.

6. Be specific

Goals are useless if they are not specific. Don't set your long-term career goal as something vague, such as "helping people" or "making a lot of money." You should express your goal in specific terms, such as "I will be a surgeon" or "I will be an aid worker in Africa" or "I will run my own company."

The same is true for other categories of goals. Don't say, "I want to get good grades." Set a specified standard: "I will achieve a 3.00 grade point average this semester" or "I will get straight As in my science courses."

The more exact you are, the easier it is to measure your progress. It's also a better way to tell when you're done and can move on to the next goal. A specific long-term goal is more inspiring for the future. A specific immediate goal on your to-do list is more inspiring for today because you can cross it off your list and know you are one small step closer to that wonderful future.

It's a funny thing about life; if you refuse to accept anything but the best, you very often get it.

Somerset Maugham

Never, never, never, never give up.

Sir Winston Churchill

We all make mistakes,
but everyone makes
different mistakes.

  Ludwig van Beethoven

In the middle of
difficulty lies opportunity.

  Albert Einstein

If you fall down seven
times, get up eight times

  Daruma Daishi

7. Include actions

Setting the goal isn't enough by itself. You need to commit to the actions required to achieve your goal. The specific actions required to achieve long-term goals become the small goals you set for yourself this month or this week or on today's to-do list.

8. Expect failure

If you find a path with no obstacles, it probably doesn't lead anywhere. That which is truly challenging and inspirational is rarely easy. Don't give up just because you are not immediately successful or the path seems too difficult. If your dreams still feel right for you and still inspire you, your failure should be nothing more than a message that you need to reevaluate your action plan. Learn from your failures, but don't let them determine your life's direction.

9. Rewrite, revise, revisit, review — CHANGE

Setting goals, especially in the long and intermediate terms, does not set your life in stone. Take time to review your goals and revise them a little or change them completely if necessary. Develop the flexibility of mind to reevaluate your current goals if your path leads you into contact with better, more inspiring goals.

Change the priorities, change the long-term goals, change the intermediate route to the long-term goals, change the strategy for getting to the intermediate goal. It's all fair game for change. You're in control. When your interests, loves, desires change, alter your goals. Don't feel defeated if you change because you want to. But make sure you set new goals before you start to drift.

10. Link your goals

There should be a thread by which you can trace the direct relationship between today's activity and your longest-term dreams and goals. For example, if your dream is to be a judge, you have to have a long-term goal to be a lawyer, which means your intermediate goal has to be to get into law school, which means your short-term goal has to be to get good marks this semester, which means your goal for today must be to read 25 pages in your history text. Do you see the chain of connection?

When the action you are taking right now is directly supporting your long-term goal and is lifting you incrementally toward it, you are experiencing the power of goal setting as a motivator, focusing agent, and cure for procrastination.

11. Enjoy the journey

Goal setting is a tool. It's a vital and incredibly valuable tool, but it is no more than that. Don't become so obsessively goal-oriented that you ignore the joy of the journey and rewards of reveling in the characteristics of the person you become on your way to that goal. Often it is those people who focus on the path of mastery rather than the journey's end who achieve the most in life.

c. Goal setting and studying

The principles in section **b.** above can be applied to setting goals for all aspects of your life. Here are some examples of how you can use them to help motivate you in your studying and keep you on track for achieving the results you want.

1. Long-term goals

Long-term goals are your dreams. The reason you are studying today has to be linked to some dream about how you want to spend your life. For some people, the mere exercise of their minds and the expansion of their genius potential is enough motivation to study. They have the long-term goal of enjoying being the best person they can be, and they see academic study for its own sake as a way to achieve that goal.

Most people believe that is worthy, but they have something more concrete in mind as a primary motivator. It is usually a career goal — something that will last much of their adult lives. Nevertheless, the long-term goals that work best in motivating the student are still those that are inspirational. What vision of your life really grabs your imagination? Imagine your life ten years from now. What do you want to be doing?

If your long-term goal is to be a doctor or entrepreneur or musician because that is what your heart tells you is right for you, you will be well motivated on a daily basis. On the other hand, if you set these as your goals because it's what your parents want, or what you feel you ought to do as a career, but you personally aren't sure, you will have a more difficult time keeping your daily studying on track.

If you always do what you always did, you'll always get what you always got!

Verne Hill

It has long since come to my attention that people of accomplishment rarely sat back and let things happen to them. They went out and happened to things.

Adam Smith

Destiny is not a matter of chance, it is a matter of choice; it is not a thing to be waited for, it is a thing to be achieved.

   William Jennings Bryan

Set long-term goals that inspire and uplift you. They should send a shiver of anticipation through your body when you think of them. Have some reminder of them in front of you while you study.

2. Intermediate goals

Intermediate goals are usually for three to five years in the future and are one of the keys to achieving your long-term goals. For example, if you want to be a doctor, a necessary intermediate goal is getting into medical school.

3. Short-term goals

The steps toward your intermediate goal are a series of short-term goals, usually for six months to two years in the future. For example, if medical school admission requires an undergraduate degree with a 3.00 grade point average, you will have a series of short-term goals that consists of earning that average each semester or each academic year.

4. Immediate goals

You can't get straight As, or a 3.00 grade point average for that matter, if you don't get today's homework assignment done. Immediate goals are those that lead to the accomplishment of short-term goals. This is where the principle of "divide and conquer" comes into play most strongly.

Each short term can be daunting by itself. Even some of the more immediate goals can feel that way. If you divide each goal into smaller portions until you have a list of tasks that can each be accomplished in 30 minutes to an hour, you have created a powerful procrastination weapon.

Think about it. If you have only one hour to work on your term paper, which of the following tasks will be easier to start and will let you feel successful about doing it?

   (a) Do some work on your 20-page essay,

   or

   (b) Revise the outline for the middle section of
        your 20-page essay.

The big difference is that the first statement is so vague that you could stare at the catalogue computer in the library for five minutes and claim to have "done some work" on the essay. You could also work for six hours and still not actually have completed a specific goal on the way to finishing it.

The second statement achieves something valuable toward the completion of the project, as well as giving you the feeling of completing a relevant, planned task. A series of 15 to 20 mini-tasks might be part of the plan for completing the otherwise monstrous 20-page paper. The end result is a finished essay and the chance to experience 15 to 20 successes along the way.

5. To-do lists

When you write down your immediate goals (remember, you always write your goals), and put them in priority order, you have created a to-do list for today's studying. Every immediate study goal that becomes part of your to-do list must be properly constructed and must —

- be **specific**,
- be **reasonable** (can be done in 30 to 60 minutes),
- be **verifiable** or measurable (you can tell when you're finished), and
- have a **reward** at the end.

The greatest discovery of my generation is that a human being can alter his life by altering his attitudes of mind.

William James

Rewards are important, and they can take a variety of forms. Free time, food, movies, and reading are all typical rewards for meeting study goals. There is no shame in bribing yourself if that is what it takes to get some things done.

Most often the best reward is writing a list of specific, reasonable, measurable goals for the day and watching them get crossed off as you finish each one. It feels good to see that list of accomplishments and relish the sensation of being that much closer to your long-term goals.

9.

Time management

a. Controlling your study time — it's simple!

Well . . . the concept is pretty simple. Putting it into action isn't always easy. If effective management of time was easy, there wouldn't be a need for this chapter or for the dozens of books that provide advice, strategies, and systems for controlling your time.

My personal attitude is that complex time management systems are not only unnecessary, but they also create more problems than they solve because they use so much time being maintained. Adopt a simple time management approach by doing a few basic things very well and attacking some of the symptoms that high-concept time management systems fail to deal with effectively.

Most time management problems are symptoms of problems in other fundamental areas, such as preparation, goal setting, motivation, and concentration — which just happen to be the subjects of other chapters in this book. Read and reread those chapters, put the strategies into action, and you will discover most of your so-called time management problems will disappear.

Here is all you need to know about time management. Each item assumes studying as a priority, but you can adapt this list to any part of your life.

- Know what your priorities are.
- Spend time on your priorities.
- Set proper study goals.

- Don't waste time on things that are nonessential to studying activities.
- Make a basic schedule. Don't get complex or rigid.
- Keep a calendar of important events (such as exams, essay due dates, birthdays).
- Use the power of lists.
- Develop your concentration.
- Be flexible. If one approach isn't working, change it.
- Do it right the first time.

That's really all there is to it. Most of these issues are covered in other chapters, but it is worth reviewing some of the essential elements in the context of effective use of time. There are also some new concepts to think about adding to your toolbox of skills.

Dost thou love Life?

Then do not squander

Time; for that's the stuff

Life is made of.

Benjamin Franklin

Remember, good time management for a student is not about creating an intricate schedule that makes you account for every second of your day. It is about one simple choice: either you will control your school work, or it will control you. Good time management puts you in control.

b. Setting priorities

The essence of time management is trying to be efficient. There is nothing more naturally efficient than spending time doing what is related to your goals and priorities. In chapter 7, principle 4 for study success tells you to spend time on what matters. The first step in that decision is to actually know what matters to you. Read and review chapter 8 to understand the power and necessity of goal setting as the foundation of good time management.

c. Dealing with procrastination

Procrastination is the

thief of time.

Edward Young

Everybody puts things off. It's basic human nature to avoid pain and pursue pleasure. Even if watching TV while ignoring your studying will bring long-term pain and result in missing the long-term pleasure of success, it is the short-term pleasure/pain dichotomy that has the most influence. At that moment, watching *Beverly Hills 90210* seems more pleasurable than doing your math homework — even though the longer-term may be an F in math and a life on welfare where you can't even afford a TV.

How do you overcome this vicious cycle? Simple. Not easy, but certainly simple. There are five things you must do to overcome procrastination each time it threatens to rob you of your study time: you must prepare, set study goals, imagine the pain, imagine the pleasure, and give yourself permission to procrastinate on some things.

Try the following techniques for two weeks and you will see a sharp decline in the amount of study time you waste. Remember to review the skills and concepts from earlier chapters.

1. Prepare

Read chapter 4 again and follow the suggestions given there. Having an inviting place to study, as well as a planned set of steps for preparation — almost like a ritual — make it more likely you will choose to sit down and begin studying.

2. Set study goals

Remember the characteristics of good study goals: specific, reasonable, verifiable, and rewardable. If you have a written set of easy-to-start and soon-to-be-finished study goals, procrastination is much less likely. It's the huge daunting tasks that are easy to put off. A small goal that will be finished in 30 minutes and will be a contribution to a larger goal is one of the best procrastination beaters.

3. Imagine the pain

Procrastination diverts you from what you should be doing. It distracts you from achieving the things you really want to do. It doesn't take long for this to build up and eat away at you. It robs you of the joy of achievement. It steals your confidence and mastery of yourself. The things not done pile up and you are filled with anxiety and dread.

Each time you find yourself procrastinating, pause and imagine the pain of avoiding what you should be doing. Make it real. Use all your senses and memories of past procrastination and make all the sensations as intense as you can. Use some of the elementary visualization techniques described in chapter 4.

4. Imagine the pleasure

Immediately after giving yourself a realistic dose of the pain of not acting on your goals, treat yourself to some pleasure. Use the same imaginative power to feel the exhilaration of achieving your long-term goal. How will it feel to get an A in this course? What will it mean to you to get accepted to law school? How proud will you feel? Imagine seeing your name on the office door when you get your dream job.

Feel the freedom and pride and wonder at the power of setting a goal in your heart and finally achieving it. Mentally review the chain of events that ties that inspiring goal to today's study tasks and you have a power motivator to get yourself to your desk NOW!

5. Give yourself permission to procrastinate on some things

Life is filled with things that should be done and priorities change from week to week and day to day. At times in your life it's okay to procrastinate on some things. If there are items on your to-do list, such as cut the grass, paint the house, or give the car a tune-up, give yourself permission to let those slide sometimes. If you have met your study goals for the day, it's perfectly all right to place your reward for that achievement ahead of other things that have to get done.

Be reasonable about this. If neglecting the car means you won't be able to get to work or school in the morning, you should get to it. But remember, if you've done the important things, don't worry so much about the other tasks — for now. If they need to be done, they will eventually become a top priority and you won't ignore them (e.g., put them off until the essay is finished, or until after your last mid-term exam).

Even such is Time, that

takes in trust

Our youth, our joys, our

all we have,

And pays us but with

age and dust.

Sir Walter Raleigh

d. Doing it right the first time

Aside from watching TV and shopping, the biggest thief of your valuable time is doing a sloppy job when you do get down to work. If you can't be bothered to do it right the first time, when will you be motivated to do it over? What a colossal waste of time and effort.

Think about it. It takes effort to do a lousy job. It doesn't take that much more to do it right. It really doesn't. Make the effort to prepare yourself properly and be an active learner in all situations: reading, during lectures, in labs, in the library. Everywhere!

Being passive and unengaged in any of your study tasks is wasted time. You will retain almost nothing and you will either have to start over when it is time to prepare for the final exam, or you will fail the course. Both situations mean you have wasted the time you spent doing poor studying and learning. Why not put 30% more effort into it and earn 100% more results?

Doing it right the first time is one of the best time management techniques you can learn. That's what this book is all about — giving you skills and strategies for getting the most out of the same amount of study time.

e. Making schedules

Making schedules is at the heart of most time management advice. There are some very complex and expensive systems out there. Many study skills books provide examples of scheduling systems that look more involved than charting new galaxies.

Life for a student, whether full time or part time, is complex, and schedules are necessary. But remember, you must create one that is your tool, not your tyrant. A good tool will be used again and again. A tyrant will be overthrown and forgotten.

A good schedule does not shackle your life. A good schedule is not carved in stone. A good schedule is a flexible tool that does not make its user feel like a failure if it gets violated. Here are the elements you should use to create good schedules for achieving your study goals.

Next week there can't be any crisis. My schedule is full.

Henry Kissinger

1. Make a weekly master schedule

At the beginning of each semester, make a master schedule of everything in your life that is a fixed item. Your class times, seminars, labs, and part-time job hours are all examples of fixed elements in your schedule.

2. Add study time to your schedule

Using the principles in sections **i.** and **j.** below, block off large sections of your day that are exclusively reserved for studying. Remember to take account of when you are most alert for studying and to make use of any open times before and after classes.

3. Add nonstudy items to your schedule

If there are other important, but lower priority, parts of your life that are fixed or best done at certain times, plug them into the schedule after you have made your weekly master schedule and blocked off your study time in it. Examples of nonstudy items are regular exercise, such as a walk or swimming. Others might be recreation or nonacademic classes, such as karate, piano lessons, or learning sign language.

If the best time for a walk is in the late afternoon when your study alertness is low anyway, put a walk in as a scheduled activity. That signals to you to be most efficient by using time that is useless for learning for something physically beneficial. Nonacademic courses are fixed, so they have to go into the schedule. Remember not to interfere with the fixed academic and study sessions. Everything else, no matter how interesting, is of secondary importance and has to be worked around your #1 priority — studying.

4. Be flexible and persistent

Don't give up if it isn't working. Make changes to your approach, but do not stop working toward a schedule that works for you.

5. Leave some blank space

Why do most schedules fail? Because they are too full. Use the schedule to program your fixed items and to block off time for nonfixed priority activity (in this case, studying). Do not attempt to schedule every aspect of your life. Schedules that contain items like "2:47 p.m. to 3:06 p.m. — RELAX" are doomed to fail very quickly.

Once you have accounted for all the necessary parts of your life, including adequate study time, leave significant blank spaces in your schedule. That's your "free" time. Do anything you want with it. Waste it if you like. Do other things from your other lists, such as write a thank-you letter to your grandmother or buy a birthday present for your sister. You can even study if you want to, but you don't have to. Experiment to find what are good, feasible blocks to keep free. Try to be consistent once you find them. Keep Tuesday and Thursday evenings free. Keep all day Saturday or Sunday completely unscheduled. Be creative and flexible.

Sample #1 shows how a weekly master schedule might look.

f. Using to-do lists

Making daily to-do lists has been mentioned in other chapters. Review chapter 8, which shows to-do lists in the context of goal setting. A daily list of things to do is nothing more than a list of small, immediate goals.

You must have a written list of study "to-do's" if your study schedule is going to work. The best weapons against procrastination and poor concentration are a scheduled study time and a list of specific things to do once you sit down at the appointed time.

What appears at the top of your to-do list depends on your class schedule and your calendar of important events. If you have a lecture two hours from now in which the professor will assume you have read chapter 4 in your textbook, your priority for the study session is obvious. If you have an exam scheduled next week that will cover five chapters you have not read yet, your priority for today should be to cover some portion of that material.

If you have a clear picture of what's coming up in your academic life, you will be able to adjust your to-do priorities accordingly.

Men talk of killing time, while time quietly kills them.

Dion Boucicault

SAMPLE #1
CLASS AND STUDY SCHEDULE

	M	T	W	Th	F	S	Su
7:30							
8:30	Biology	↑	Biology	↑	Biology		
9:30	English	STUDY	English	STUDY	English		
10:30	Study		Study		Study		
11:30	History		History		History		↑
12:30	Lunch	↓	Lunch	↓	Run		STUDY
1:30	Study / SWIM / Lunch		Study / SWIM / Lunch		Lunch / Study		
2:30	MATH	Biology LAB	MATH		MATH Tutorial		
3:30							↓
4:30	Run	↓	Run				
5:30							
6:30	Dinner	Dinner	Dinner	Dinner	Dinner		Dinner
7:30	Study	↑	PSYC Lecture	↑			↑
8:30	Study	STUDY		STUDY			STUDY
9:30	Study	↓	↓	↓			↓

108

g. Using calendars

Calendars, like schedules, make use of your visual intelligence to give you a spatial depiction of your future. Put all deadlines, exams, and other important dates on a calendar and keep it in front of you when you work.

It is important to use these key dates as reference points for planning your daily work. For example, if the mid-term exam is two weeks away and you have five chapters to read and the total number of pages is 88, you plan accordingly. Work backward from the actual exam date as follows:

- Allow one full day for review and active output practice immediately before the exam.
- Allow two full days for consolidation and making review notes and mind maps.
- Allow a day of grace to finish the reading.
- Use the remaining days to get all the reading done in time to be able to do some proper exam preparation. In this example, you have ten days to do so.
- Determine how many pages you must read and make notes on each day. In this example, you must read and make notes on an average of 8.8 pages each and every day. And, therefore, for the next ten days, you will have a specific to-do item on your list telling you to read and make notes on 9 pages of that textbook. If you leave that course until it is only one week until the exam, obviously the amount of work in the preceding days is much more.

Keep your calendar up-to-date and use it to develop your daily goals and priorities.

Sample #2 shows an example of a calendar of important dates.

h. Implementing the principle of divide and conquer

The example above shows you the principle of divide and conquer in action. A total of 88 pages may seem daunting, but the longer the lead time you have (or give yourself by starting sooner!), the smaller the tasks you actually have to complete each day. Working through 9 pages a day doesn't seem so bad. Review this principle in chapter 7 and use it every day.

SAMPLE #2
CALENDAR OF IMPORTANT DATES

M	T	W	Th	F	S	Su
			1	2	3	4
5	6 Biology LAB #3 DUE	7 PSYC QUIZ	8	9 English In-Class Essay	10	11 MOM's BIRTHDAY
12	13	14	15	16	17	18
19	20 Biology LAB #4 DUE	21	22	23 FINISH HISTORY Essay OUTLINE	24	25
26 History mid-term	27	28 Biology mid-term PSYC QUIZ	29	30 MATH mid-term	31	

i. Using fractions of time

Not all the best study time is to be found in the nice large blocks that you set out in your ideal schedule. Some of the prime time to do superlearning is during the bits and pieces of time you throw away every day. If you commit yourself to reclaiming some of this time, you can double and triple your learning rate.

Make flash cards or one-page lists of vocabulary words, rules of grammar, math formulas, or dates. If you are studying chemistry, get a laminated copy of the periodic table of elements.

Keep these flash cards or short lists with you at all times. Take them out and review them quickly when —

- drying your hair or shaving (put them up against the mirror),
- toweling off after stepping out of the shower,
- eating your breakfast (prop two or three up against your cereal box),
- waiting for the bus (but not while driving),
- while stopped for construction delays (but not at stop lights),
- waiting in line for anything — at the bank, in the bookstore, in the cafeteria,
- waiting those five minutes before your next class, or
- any time you just don't feel like any other kind of sustained study.

It doesn't have to be much work: just two, three, or four cards, just a few items on the list. But it's amazing what you can accomplish by doing this. You are refreshing your memory by familiarization, reviewing, rehearsing, and practicing active output all in the space of a few minutes. Do this constantly and you will gain hours of valuable study time each week.

Another important use of the time immediately before and immediately following classes is to review your class notes. These pieces of time are the most criminally wasted in a student's life.

Most people stare mindlessly into space or chat aimlessly while waiting for class to begin. You could be activating your prior knowledge by reviewing your notes from previous lectures. Remember chapter 4 on preparation — it is vital to

I knew a gentleman who was so good a manager of his time that he would not even lose that small portion of it which the calls of nature obliged him to pass in the necessary-room; but gradually went through all the Latin poets in those moments.

Lord Chesterfield

effective learning that your preparation include some kind of subject-specific warm-up for your brain. Use this time wisely and you will get much more out of each lecture and much more of it will be retained.

After class, don't just "veg out" somewhere or go off to the cafeteria for coffee. There's nothing wrong with tuning out to relax or joining your classmates after a lecture, but don't waste the valuable learning time immediately after the class. If you take five to ten minutes right afterward to review your notes, visualize the lecture in your mind's eye and hear the words again, and then add new information to your notes, you can sometimes double what you've learned from that class. That's right! Double the learning with an extra five to ten minutes.

The key element is doing it immediately after the class ends. Not an hour later or the next day. Right after class! After you're finished, go join your friends for coffee or a beer — you've earned it then and it's not lost time.

j. Being aware of your alertness cycles

Plan to study when you are most alert. Schedule other activities or leave open time when you are less mentally sharp.

This seems painfully obvious, but you would be amazed at the number of people who do not consider this factor when scheduling their study time. Perhaps you are such a person. It is not a good idea to plug study time into your schedule simply because there is a space there. If you are not very alert at 7:00 a.m., don't try to force yourself to study then. It just won't work. If your energy sags in the late afternoon, plan on doing something else at that time, because studying will be a waste of time.

If you don't know what your alertness cycle is like, make the effort to pay attention to that for at least a week. Evaluate your energy level and how alert you feel at different times in the day. If you just cannot keep your eyes open after reading one page, but everyone else seems to be able to work, don't worry. Just keep at it until you find the periods of highest alertness and adjust your study schedule accordingly (where practical).

If you cannot find enough time when you are alert enough to study, you may have to do something to fix the situation.

Your course load might be too heavy for the time you have available. If you are using your highest alert periods for a job, you will have to cut back or change your hours — or cut back your school commitments. You can't have both if your day isn't left with enough study time.

You can also try to expand your alert periods by working in three areas of behavior. First, make certain you get enough sleep. Lack of proper sleep is the major reason for mental dullness and lack of efficient study time. Second, get some exercise. Exercise has been proven to increase the levels of those chemicals in the brain that keep you alert and focused for learning. Finally, prepare yourself. You can boost your energy and alertness by following a proper preparation sequence. Review chapter 4.

k. Using lists

The use of study to-do lists has already been discussed. Their value can be transferred to other aspects of your life and help you control the many small things that interrupt concentration and end up wasting your time. It is much easier to get down to studying at the appointed time and concentrate fully if other things do not intrude.

Important personal tasks and basic daily chores should be listed. Keep such tasks and chores recorded on a list. That is part of the secret of staying in control of the time thieves. With a schedule that shows committed time and free time, a calendar showing important events and deadlines, and list of tasks, you can see the enemies in front of you. There are no surprises, no memory lapses resulting in emergencies, and no anxiety from feeling out of control.

It sounds too simple to work, but the power is amazing. Try it. Start making lists of all the letters to write, presents to buy, personal chores to be done, shopping to do, etc. It will be a long list, but do not be discouraged by this. At least you now have control. If you know you won't lose control of any of these tasks (not too many anyway — after all, you're only human). The relief that comes from writing things down will be translated into fewer excuses to keep you from hitting the books when scheduled study time comes around.

There is time for many words, and there is also time for sleep.

Homer

I. Squandering time versus valid "down time"

Time, the devourer of

all things.

Ovid

Time is squandered if you do low-priority things during periods set aside to work on your high-priority goals. If you do those same time-wasting activities during the blank time in your schedule, there's no problem.

Cleaning the fridge or reading a trashy novel when you should be studying your medieval literature is evil time theft. But if you do those things when you had nothing else planned, it's okay because that was "down time" anyway.

If you don't want school work to invade your "free" time, then do the academic stuff when it appears in your schedule. That leaves the blank space in your schedule free for anything you want — GUILT FREE. Doing frivolous, work-avoiding activity when you should be studying isn't as much fun as it could be because there is a ton of guilt that comes with it. Doing it when you've earned the time away from your books relieves you of any guilt.

10.

Information source 1: Study reading

a. Different kinds of reading

There are different kinds of reading. Scanning the menu at a restaurant is reading. Skimming through the phone book searching for a particular name is reading. Glancing through a magazine while waiting for your turn with the dentist is reading. Devouring every word of a best-selling thriller is reading even though you will not remember much beyond the barest outline of the plot two days after you finish the book. And "reading" is also the label given to the process in which we engage when we try to understand, learn, and retain complex material published in printed form.

All these activities are called reading, but they have very different purposes and results. As a successful student, one of the most useful distinctions you can make is to understand the different kinds of reading and their purposes. They are all valid, but not equally useful at all times. A detailed analysis and understanding of the phone book is not only time consuming, but its content doesn't really warrant that kind of intensity. The plot of a restaurant menu is rarely engrossing enough to read at the same level as a well-written political biography. Skimming your textbook like it was a phone book will not leave you with much information to impart on your final exam.

Scanning is a useful skill for looking at the results of a search of your library's on-line catalogue. You will want to skim through the index of your textbook if you want one particular reference. But 99% of your reading as a student in formal school settings will be slow, detailed study reading. Do not confuse this process with any other kind of reading

b. The purpose of study reading

He has only half learned the art of reading who has not added to it the more refined art of skipping and skimming.

Lord Balfour

Study reading is the slowest, most intricate of the various kinds of reading. Its purpose is to absorb and retain material presented in many different kinds of printed formats, but usually in the form of a textbook.

Your mind will understand and register a lot of material when you skim and scan, but the purpose is limited and these items are usually stored temporarily in your short-term memory. For example, your eyes will scan dozens of names in a phone book, and your brain will retain the seven digits of the number you want to dial. But how often do you remember those names or that phone number even ten minutes after you make the call? That data has disappeared from your short-term memory.

In study reading, you need to concentrate on each word and let it register in your brain. You need to work with the material in the many different, focused ways that will make it part of your long-term memory.

If you have unrealistic expectations about the speed and ease with which you can properly study your textbooks, you will very quickly get frustrated and set yourself on the road to exam disaster. Do not expect to go fast. Your texts cannot be read like novels or directories. Start out by knowing that effective study reading is slow, sometimes tedious, hard work.

On the other hand, study reading is the most satisfying of all reading. All other forms serve a purpose, but only study reading changes you. Aside from the obvious medium-term benefit of passing exams and getting better grades (and the self-confidence that comes with excellent results), don't underestimate the power of knowledge that you accumulate as course after course of information becomes part of you.

c. What about speed reading?

Forget "speed reading" as a solution to the mountain of reading you can be faced with in school and some training courses. Stay away from any book, course, or teacher that claims to be able to give you a reading speed of thousands of words per minute with full comprehension. It is physically impossible to train yourself to read faster than 400 to 500 words per minute. The average student will read at a speed of 250 to 350 words per minute. That's it! Any faster than that and you are no longer study reading and comprehension is compromised.

No "breakthrough" technology can overcome that. Don't be fooled or cheated by such claims. Save your money and your time. Get down to the hard work of study reading.

If you have a genuine reading difficulty, see a specialist. Reading disabilities such as dyslexia are not a barrier to learning and study success, but you do need to be properly diagnosed. Proper treatment and training can help open the same doors to knowledge and success available to most people.

If you are just a typical lazy reader with bad habits, there are simple techniques you can use to train yourself to become more efficient (see section **e.** below). There is no such thing as speed reading to study and remember. *There are no short cuts.*

He [Napoleon] read so fast that a book lasted him scarcely one hour, and at Saint Helena, a servant was kept busy carrying away armfuls of finished books which only the day before had been brought from the shelves.

Emil Ludwig

d. Reading methods or systems

Using a well thought-out reading "method" will aid your study reading. A commercial reading "system" will not. These reading systems are usually just speed-reading courses that have been tarted up a bit. But the same objections as discussed above apply.

A method is an approach that uses certain basic principles for learning and retaining material from a textbook. However, the principles should be adapted to the student, the particular textbook, the subject, and the circumstances. Advocates of a reading or speed-reading system will claim that you can apply its rigid rules to all reading situations with astounding results.

Again, there are no short cuts. But there are a lot of good things you can do to improve the effectiveness of your study reading.

e. Principles for getting the most from your study reading

1. Map out your route

One of the worst things you can do as a study reader is to open your book and begin detailed reading on the very first page without any preliminary work. This is like setting out on a long journey without looking at a map to see where you are going and what you are likely to encounter along the way. It is also like trying to build a house without blueprints or any idea of what you want the house to look like.

Your goal should be to develop the habit of "surveying" or "previewing" each textbook and each chapter within that textbook. You will develop the obvious but rarely practiced skill of having a precise road map or framework in your head before you start detailed reading.

Remember the sample memory exercise in chapter 5? The principle there is that it is easier to remember a list of items if you know in advance what the categories are. Your memory works by association and by combining unknown new things with known factors already stored in long-term memory. Therefore, the more detailed your list of landmarks on the road map, the more chance you have to store the new, unfamiliar material that you encounter in your reading.

Here is an example of how to survey a textbook chapter and create a valuable road map for the dense material to come later. The single most important principle in surveying is to make use of many clues, cues, and memory hooks that have already been supplied for you, but which are usually glossed over as irrelevant or useless. They are *very* useful.

Step 1   Read the title and think about what is going to be discussed in the chapter. This is an obvious but often ignored first step. It is a technique of activating prior knowledge.

Step 2   Look in the table of contents for the book. If there is a summary of the chapter or an outline of the main points, read it carefully and take 30 seconds to think about it and let it sink in.

Step 3

If there is a summary or outline at the beginning or end of the chapter, repeat Step 2.

Step 4

If there is a set of review or discussion questions, read them. Use them as a set of clues as to what the author feels is important in the chapter. Why waste time trying to figure it out if someone will tell you? Studying should be hard work; that's how you learn. But that doesn't mean you should ignore assistance when it's offered to you.

Step 5

Read the introductory and concluding sections or paragraph. These are also often summaries of the content and indicators of what is important.

Step 6

Read all the major headings. Think about how the chapter is structured and what basic divisions are made in the information.

Step 7

Read all the subheadings and sub-subheadings. These indicate significant subject areas within a major heading.

Step 8

Read the first sentence of each paragraph. This is usually the topic sentence and the best cue to the content of the paragraph.

Step 9

Examine all graphics. Look at all the pictures, graphs, maps, and so on. Read all captions carefully. Your goal is to understand what the graphics are telling you and how they fit into the structure of the chapter. Don't be surprised if after doing Steps 1 through 8, you actually understand quite a bit about the graphics.

Step 10

This step is vital. If you skip it, you will have wasted most of the time you spent surveying.

Take 60 to 90 seconds to review and rehearse the main points of the chapter and the important material contained in it. It's best to do this in writing. Write it out as fast as you can, using key words and phrases. There are no points for neatness or complete sentences. The goal is not to create lasting notes. What you want to do is consolidate the framework before you go on to detailed reading. Do this. It is important.

This whole process should take no longer than 5 to 15 minutes (depending on the length of the chapter). Yet, in that time, you can actually absorb and retain as much as 50% to 60% of the important information in the chapter — just by using the structure of the typical textbook to your advantage.

A book published by Self-Counsel Press is an excellent type of book on which to practice this technique. Try it on this one.

2. Use a flexible method

Steps 1 to 10 described above give an example of a useful method of using the principles of previewing, but it is not a lockstep system. Remember to be flexible in your application of the method. Adapt it to the way different texts are structured.

You can even adapt this method to different purposes. For instance, use these ideas to preview entire books to determine how useful they might be for your term paper.

3. Be deliberate: Do it right the first time

Study reading requires a high level of focus and concentration. This applies to surveying and previewing as well. Do not attempt either until you are in the proper state of mind — remember to prepare yourself — to work hard. Reading as a serious student is not something you can do passively. It will be a waste of time. Make a commitment to have each reading session productive and effective. It will save you time in the long run to do it right the first time.

4. Be active

The information in the books won't come to you. You must go and take it.

Good study reading is active, not passive. You cannot simply have your eyes run over the words and expect to be taught something. The responsibility is yours to do the learning. Take the knowledge and information that is contained in the written material, and make it yours. That takes hard, active work.

There are many techniques for starting out your reading in an alert, active state and staying that way while you read. Here are three of the easiest and the best.

(a) Activate prior knowledge

Every time you sit down to read, you must take a few moments to review what you already know. This is a way of warming up your memory and activating as many "memory pegs" as possible on which to hang new information.

Survey or preview of a book or chapter is a kind of prior knowledge activation. Doing this type of exercise before each reading session provides a better framework for the material you want to keep and store in your long-term memory.

This is one of those little steps that may seem annoying and tempting to skip when your energy is low or you are particularly pressed for time and anxious to get down to serious reading. Try not to give in to the temptation, because it is the cumulative effect of these "little steps" that makes the difference between barely passing and getting As.

(b) Question and conclude

One of the best methods of remaining active while you read is to develop the habits of asking questions and drawing conclusions. The more questions you ask of the text, the more answers you find. It is a peculiarity of memory that you tend to remember answers to your own questions more often than you recall information that came to you unsolicited. An answer to your own questions is something you sought out. It makes a difference.

There is a similar effect with making conclusions as you go along. Make up your mind about what this all means and test it against what comes next in the chapter. Then information tends to take on one of two characteristics. Either it proves you wrong and forces you to change your conclusion, or it supports what you believed all along. Both situations mean that the information is no longer a neutral fact to be remembered. Instead it is transformed into more evidence for your position or a contradiction that forces you to rethink things.

(c) Anticipate

Try to guess what is going to come next and how it will relate to what you have just read. As with questioning and concluding, anticipating changes the nature of the next passage from neutral data into an answer to a challenge you have set for yourself.

It is chiefly through books that we enjoy the intercourse with superior minds.

William Ellery Channing

The art of reading is among other things the art of adopting that pace the author has set. Some books are fast and some are slow, but no book can be understood if it is taken at the wrong speed.

Mark Van Doren

5. Vary speed to suit purpose

Most of your reading will be at a slow pace so you can read each word and to allow time for you to absorb what you are trying to learn. But don't be afraid to vary your normal speed if the situation warrants it. Sometimes it's okay to skim, scan, and skip over material if you have made a conscious decision to do this based on rational grounds.

Going quickly over a section because your eyes are tired, you can't concentrate, the material is boring, or the print is too small is not a good decision.

6. Make the material part of you

Making the material part of you is the desirable and logical conclusion of the process of active reading. If you are active enough before, during, and after your reading, what you read becomes a part of you and, therefore, available for recall during an examination.

There is no better way to make information part of you than by making notes as you read. It must become as much a part of your study reading as moving your eyes and thinking.

Notice that the phrase is "make" notes, not "take" notes. It is an important distinction. "Taking" notes is a passive activity. You are merely recording data to be learned later — the learning is postponed. When you "make" notes, you are actively creating something of your own and engaging in learning immediately.

Good note making is NOT —

- simply copying out passages,
- merely highlighting sections to be learned later,
- just underlining words without thinking, or
- making mindless doodles.

Good note making involves —

- **thinking** about the material before recording anything,
- **writing** short condensations of passages in your own words,
- **writing** key words in the margins of the textbook,
- **underlining** or highlighting only key words (and no more), and
- drawing simple **diagrams** or graphs of your own devising.

As you read, think about the words and decide —

- what to make notes on,
- what to ignore; what to leave out,
- how to make the notes,
- what key words or symbols or shorthand you will use,
- what you will do to make your notes memorable, and
- how this note relates to your other notes and reading.

All this thinking and deciding will enhance learning beyond any level you previously achieved, because this kind of mental activity makes the material part of you.

You also need to tell yourself that you are learning with each step. It is happening with each moment of focus and high-quality concentration. Don't look on reading and note making as preliminary activities, with the real learning coming later. If you convince yourself that NOW is the learning moment, it will happen. It doesn't come later when you are preparing for the exam. "Later" is for review, rehearsal, and output practice. Make a commitment to this attitude and you will be amazed by the improvement in your learning — and how short a time it can actually take.

7. Check your physical environment

Make sure you follow the lighting requirements for good study conditions set out in chapter 4. Low level of light, light flicker, and no alternative light sources are all common causes of eye strain and doziness. Attention to proper lighting can greatly

I would advise you to read with a pen in your hand, and enter in a little book short hints of what you find . . . for this will be the best method of imprinting such particulars in your memory, where they will be ready, on some future occasion. . . .

Benjamin Franklin

enhance your study reading endurance and the quality of learning.

If the air where you are reading is too warm or too stuffy, you will have problems with your concentration. Again, follow the recommendations in chapter 4 about proper air temperature and ventilation.

8. Eliminate roving eye syndrome

One of the major mechanical problems with reading speed can be dealt with simply and easily, but it takes discipline. You will be pushed outside your comfort zone.

If you believe your study reading speed is slower than it should be, take a few minutes to analyze your reading pattern. Try to identify sources of distraction, lapses in concentration (mind wandering), and where your eye travels. If you observe that you often reread lines several times and your eye tends to rove over the page, causing you to constantly restart your reading, you have a "wandering eye" problem. Its cause is mostly lazy reading habits which eventually become so ingrained that the problem occurs even when you are concentrating well.

Fortunately, there are easily employed techniques for retraining your eye to stay focused on the text at hand and avoid backtracking. The most common technique is to simply use your finger, pen, or pencil as a kind of "pacer." Draw your chosen guide along underneath the line of text. Force your eyes to read the text immediately above the tracer. Do this at an easy pace to begin with; you don't want to become frustrated at the beginning and give up. Even at this slow pace you will have the overwhelming feeling that you are missing something. It will feel very uncomfortable resisting your urge to backtrack. Resist it.

You can accomplish the same thing by using a ruler or recipe card. There are two ways to use such a read-pacing device. You can hold the card just above the line of text you are reading, and then slide it down to cover that line as soon as you have finished reading it. Or, you can hold the edge of the ruler or card immediately under the line you are reading. When you finish that line, slide the card so that it underlines the next line of text. In both cases, force yourself to read only what is underlined or "overlined" by the edge.

Once you have reached a moderate level of comfort with this technique, you can move on to reading like this more quickly. You don't have to do this, though. Usually, the mere act of using a guide to help prevent backtracking will be enough to keep you focused on the text. If you want to go further, use your preferred method to push yourself beyond what is comfortable. Move the pencil or card just a little bit faster than you would like for word-for-word reading. Don't go too fast, just fast enough that you feel the same level of discomfort you felt when you initiated the first stage.

Remember, there is a physical limit to the speed you can reach in study reading, so don't go overboard. Use this technique to push yourself to improve, but don't forget that if you go too fast, you will miss information, and that's a waste of time you cannot afford.

9. Consider your study time

Time is an important factor to consider in maximizing the effectiveness of your study reading. The first aspect to be aware of is your own natural alertness cycle and how it should govern when you do your most intense reading. As discussed in chapter 9, you should try to schedule your study reading sessions when you will be at your best level of alertness. Don't force yourself to do extended sessions of concentrated reading at times when you just won't be effective. It is counterproductive.

The other obvious aspect of study time is the appropriate length of time for each study reading session. As discussed in other chapters, the ideal block of study time is 30 to 45 minutes of sustained concentration. Less than that is really too fragmented and more is pushing high effectiveness limits. Remember, you want to create many beginnings and endings in your study time, so many sessions of less than an hour are better than one three-hour block.

10. Consolidate

Review, review, review. Practice activating your new knowledge. Every reading session should begin with a review of what you covered last time. Do a survey of the previous chapter; read your notes; review the margin notes of some previously read chapters. This is an activation exercise as well as an aid to consolidation.

The time to read is any time: no apparatus, no appointment of time and place is necessary. It is the only art which can be practised at any hour of the day or night, whenever the time and inclination comes that is your time for reading; in joy or sorrow, health or illness.

Holbrook Jackson

End each study reading session with a quick review of what you have just done. This doesn't need to take long, but it does need to be done. It is an amazingly simple, yet highly efficient way of solidifying information in your long-term memory.

* * *

Once you have completed this chapter, start practicing now! Survey using the technique suggested. Make a quick outline of the main points. Review them in your mind. Say them out loud. If you have been only reading this book passively until now, and you meant to become active at some point —

NOW IS THE TIME TO START.

11.

Information source 2: Class lectures

We have all had the experience of being saddled with a truly horrible teacher. Every time we went to class it was a painfully boring experience, and we left feeling that it was a waste of time. If we've been lucky, we also remember some inspiring teachers; teachers whose courses were exciting and whose classes left a lasting impression on us.

But, when it comes to how much you learn in a lecture, the quality of the instruction should be meaningless. You can waste your time just as easily in a great class as you can in a bad one. The bad teacher is not so bad that you cannot learn. A good teacher is not so good that you can rely on the high quality of the teaching to let you avoid the hard work of learning.

The responsibility for learning is yours, not the teacher's. If you develop this attitude, you can extract the learning possibilities from any class situation. Certainly it's a lot more difficult to do that when the instruction and guidance is poor, but you have the capacity to learn, independent of the teaching circumstances. Work toward being independent in this way, take on the responsibility, and you will accelerate your learning success enormously.

a. Before class

What you do before each class will have a significant impact on the quality of learning that takes place during that class. The concepts of the benefits of preparation outlined in chapter 4 are as true for classroom study as they are for private study at your desk.

1. Prepare your mind

You will get the most out of your time in classes, lectures, and seminars if you take time to prepare your mind in advance. Work on the information and your approach to it by doing the following:

- **Read** all the assigned material.
- **Review** lecture notes from previous classes.
- **Anticipate** what is coming up in this class.
- Mentally prepare your **attitude**. You're there to work, so be prepared to take in everything that is worth learning. Visualize yourself taking in the information easily, understanding it, and making notes that expand your comprehension.
- Use the **relaxation** and focusing techniques in chapter 4.

2. Prepare your body

Engaging in some physical exercise before the intense but sedentary class work enhances focus and concentration. Mild to intermediate exercise is best. You want to be active enough to stimulate the release of endorphins and increase circulation of blood (and therefore oxygen) that is so vital to superior brain function.

The kind of exercise you do depends on your starting point as an active person. For someone who does not get much exercise, a brisk walk is as intense as it should get. For the more athletic student, a longer run, swim, or aerobics class will produce the desired effect. Do not push yourself to exhaustion; that creates results that are counterproductive to sustained concentration.

Elite athletes should avoid having their intense training sessions immediately before academic lectures.

3. What you should not do before class lectures

In addition to intense, exhausting exercise, there are several other activities that can have a dramatically damaging effect on your ability to learn in the classroom:

- Eating a heavy meal immediately before the class
- Drinking alcohol
- Drinking a strong diuretic like coffee (for obvious reasons)
- Wasting the time before class
- Expecting to "be taught," as if learning is something that is done to you
- Expecting to be able to avoid required reading

b. During class

1. Attendance

Don't skip class; it's simply foolish. No matter how difficult it is to drag yourself out of bed, or how boring the lecturer may be, it is worth the effort to attend all lectures. After all, one way or another, you have paid for this time, and the material will be necessary for the final examination.

If you skip classes, you are throwing away money and wasting time because you will have to find another way to get the information you missed. You will also lose out on an opportunity to train your concentration and learning focus. In every bad class there is something to be learned — but not if you aren't there.

Remember the old adage that 85% of success in life is just showing up.

2. Where to sit and why

Unless you have a medical condition that requires you to leave the room frequently, sit in the front two or three rows in every class. There are many practical and subtle reasons for this advice:

- It's easier to hear the instructor.
- It's easier to see overheads, blackboard writing, etc.
- It's easier to concentrate on the instructor without other distractions in front of you.
- It's easier to feel like part of the class.
- It's easier to ask questions because you are closer to the teacher, and there seems to be fewer other people around to make you nervous.

- It's more difficult to leave class early.
- It's more difficult to skip class as the course goes on because you know the instructor will notice your absence.

3. Active listening

The first step in learning in class and making notes that will be meaningful is to develop "active listening" skills. Here are the features of active listening that are particularly relevant for lectures:

- Pay attention to the way your instructor has structured the lecture material. This will give you clues for where the vital information will be in later classes.
- Try to tie what you are hearing with what you already know.
- Silently question what you are hearing, and try to make conclusions about what you are learning.
- Keep an open mind about your conclusions. Be prepared to change or question your ideas when you hear something new.
- Ask questions out loud. This can be an uncomfortable thing for a naturally quiet or shy student, but do not sit in silent ignorance.
- Watch the physical movements of your instructor. You will begin to notice particular postures or gestures that accompany important points.
- Listen to the tone, timbre, and inflection of your instructor's voice. Most people will change the characteristics of their voice, either purposely or unconsciously, when they are saying something of importance.
- Learn to be an "information filter." As the course goes on, make a concerted effort to filter out what is important and focus less on the minor details of the lecture.

4. Make notes

Don't use note-taking "systems." Your objective is to record, learn, understand, and prepare material for later study. There are techniques you can use for manipulating your notes when preparing for exams, but my personal recommendation is to avoid rigid systems — especially those that require special

He who asks a question is a fool for five minutes; he who does not ask a question remains a fool forever.

Chinese proverb

books, special paper, or a lot of preparation. Your preparation time should be spent on the material, not a system.

However, just because using a specific system is not a good idea, that doesn't mean there aren't principles to follow that can make your note making better. Keep these basic precepts in mind:

- Don't attempt to take verbatim records of each lecture. That is not your purpose. You are there to learn and make a record of essential ideas and facts. Not every word is gold.

- Make most of your notes in key word form. Be selective in what you write down. If you follow the principles for what to do after the lecture (see section **c.** below), then you needn't worry about missing anything important.

- Try to find a pattern in the lecture and record the key ideas and key details in an organized fashion. The key is to use a pattern that fits the material, as well as fitting how your brain best organizes that material. Do not feel compelled to use rigid classifications systems; be flexible and creative.

- Whenever possible, make your notes in your own words. Use the instructor's exact words only when a quote is necessary or it is vital that you be precise. This will happen only occasionally.

- Copy all diagrams and graphs. Any visual supplement to the written and spoken word is special and must be recorded. It will be a stimulant to your visual intelligence — a factor often underutilized in lectures.

- Don't be afraid to be nonlinear when making connections in your notes. If you are trying hard to fit everything into an inflexible framework and something comes up in the lecture that fits in with the material recorded much earlier, what do you do? Try writing it down right where it comes in the lecture and drawing arrows to the material to which it relates. Try going back to the earlier notes and adding the new information sideways in the margin or at an angle or upside down. Be flexible and creative. (Does that sound familiar?)

- Neatness doesn't count, but clarity does! Your notes do not have to be made in your best handwriting, with proper grammar and correct spelling. You do not have to use tidy margins and spacing. What is vital, however, is that you make everything clear and easy to read. The notes do not have to be neatly indexed, but the relationship between pieces of information has to be clear. The basic rule is "neat enough to be readable and understood later, but not so obsessively ordered that it slows you down during the lecture."

- Leave a lot of blank space throughout your notes to allow space for those things you missed during class. Don't panic when you do miss something. If you use the strategies outlined in section **c.** below, you will be able to retrieve most of that information from your memory and your textbook. Your goal during the class is to leave some space on the paper to accommodate this extra material when you review the lecture and enhance your notes. Always err on the side of excess: leave more space than you think you'll need.

5. Should I tape record lectures?

Tape recording lectures is usually a bad idea. Don't waste your time or money. For most people, taping a lecture is merely a means of letting the tape recorder do the work. It is an excuse to be lazy and postpone the real effort of learning to a later time.

Also, there is the problem that not all instructors will allow their classes to be taped. If you plan to use tape recording as your primary means of remembering important material from lectures, how will you deal with a situation in which you are not permitted to use it? You're best to do the work yourself with your mind, your ears, and your pen.

Tapes can be useful if the process is not used as a crutch, but their usefulness is very limited. Tapes *can* be a helpful supplement to your written notes and can help you enhance them, but they should not be used as a primary record.

Remember, your goal is to make the information part of you, and you do that by thinking, deciding, and writing notes in your own words, not those of your teacher. If you do make tapes of your lectures, play them over again while you exercise, prepare a meal, or do your ironing.

c. After class

The work isn't over as soon as class is dismissed. You still have some learning and note making to do. The time immediately after class and the days that follow will be the most crucial to your learning what was taught in that classroom or lecture hall.

1. Immediately after class

After the class lecture you can double how much you remember, and double the effectiveness of your notes, if you do some work immediately. It is vital that you do this step right away, before the forgetting factor starts to erode your memory of the class. If you only have ten minutes between classes, USE IT. Grill your memory before any other class or activity intervenes and puts distance between you and the material from class that you still have to record. Don't just heave a sigh of relief that that particular period is over. Get to work and double your productivity.

Take the 10 or 15 or 20 minutes you have available and review your notes from the lecture you just had. While it is still fresh in your mind, add material to your notes that you may have missed the first time. Use the white space you left when the instructor was going too fast for your brain and your pen, or when you didn't quite understand the concept well enough to write it in your own words. Squeeze every last drop of detail out of your memory and write it down. Finish the sentences you couldn't finish at the time. Complete the diagrams or examples while the images are still vivid enough. Write down your impressions of what was important and what the instructor is likely to put on an exam.

Not only will you create more comprehensive notes for later study, but you will have taken your consolidation activity to another level. In addition to all the active thinking and writing you did during class, you will have added two more activity/output actions to the lecture: more thinking and more writing.

You are working smarter, because the 10 to 20 minutes you invest now is worth several hours later. That's how much extra time it would take you to get back to the same level of understanding — assuming you are able to recall the material at all.

2. Before next class

Some time before the next class in that subject, you should find time to review as much of your previous notes as possible. The ideal time is the few minutes spent waiting for class to begin. If you can't do this kind of review then because you are frantically enhancing your notes from the previous course you just finished, then do the review earlier the same day. It doesn't need to take longer than five to ten minutes. Obviously, the time will be shorter at the beginning of a course and longer as time goes on and you accumulate more material.

The goals of this kind of review are —

  (a) to constantly refresh your mind with the older material, and

  (b) to activate your prior knowledge immediately before being exposed to new material.

Make sure you hang on to what you have and prepare your mind with a hook on which to hang something new.

3. Within one week of the class

It is important to find 20 minutes each week to go back over the previous week's notes in some detail. Add more detail if it comes to you. Close your eyes and test yourself on the level of detail you can recall. Recite major points over several times. Make flash cards of important ideas and facts.

Your goal is to further consolidate the essence of the past week's lectures in your long-term memory. It doesn't take a lot of time and the review does not have to be terribly intense. Just the exposure to the information again, along with some active thinking techniques, can work wonders for your exam performance.

4. Within one month of your class

Find another 20 to 30 minutes every month for an intensive review and further revision of your notes. This is not a lot of time to find in a month for each course, but it will make a very real difference to your retention and the quality of your preparation immediately before an exam. You can do this more often, but the recommended 20 to 30 minutes per month is the minimum required to show some positive results.

Be active when you do this; do not merely read over the notes passively. Rehearse important points to yourself. Amplify points in the notes that were once vague but are now clearer to you. Write things down when you test yourself. Draw a quick mind map of the lecture. Make this short time a very active session.

You will be surprised how much you have remembered. You will also be amazed at how you are able to add to the notes.

5. Borrowing and lending notes — some pointers

If you miss a class and need to borrow someone's notes, be selective about who you ask. Try to identify the active note makers in the class. Don't waste your time borrowing poor notes.

Photocopy the borrowed notes and return them as soon as possible. These are precious to their owner and you should treat them with respect. A reliable note maker is more likely to let you borrow notes if he or she knows you are equally trustworthy. In fact, you should make the offer to photocopy and return immediately a part of your request.

Use borrowed notes as if they were a textbook or the actual lecture. Don't just put the photocopies in your notebook, or merely copy them out exactly as written by your classmate. As with all other sources of information, you must be active, alert, and willing to make the information part of you. Work with the borrowed notes.

Should you lend your notes? That depends on how generous you feel and who is doing the asking. If you are developing into a good note maker, your lecture notes become more and more valuable and it is natural to feel protective. They are very personal and customized to your mind and learning style.

If you decide you will let someone use your notes, DO NOT LET THE NOTES OUT OF YOUR POSSESSION. Offer to let the asker make photocopies, but only if he or she pays for the copying and only if you are present during the copying. This may seem overly protective, but remember that your notes are a valuable study tool and record of vital material. You should not lose control of them. Even the best of intentions on the part of the borrower can go awry and you may never see your notes again.

If the requester objects, do not be persuaded to give up possession of your notes. Sharing doesn't mean you have to be stupid about it. Conversely, do not be offended if someone sets the same conditions for giving you a copy of his or her notes.

d. Learning from audiotapes and videotapes

The increasing acceptance of alternative education formats and the advances in technology have resulted in an explosion of courses offered by teachers on tape. The University of Waterloo offers full degree programs by distance learning, with the entire course lecture series issued on audio cassettes.

Both Syracuse University and the University of London have specialized distance degree programs that give the students videotaped copies of relevant lectures. Government departments and private companies are using this technology for training employees.

There are both advantages and disadvantages to this kind of learning environment, and specific learning strategies are necessary if you are going to be successful.

1. Advantages

Here are some advantages of learning from audiotapes and videotapes:

- You can listen/watch at a time and place convenient for you.
- You can stop at any point in the taped material and return to it at any time.
- You can play the material over and over as often as you like.
- You can do other things at the same time (e.g., listen to audiotapes while you garden or do the dishes; watch videotapes while you ride an exercise bike or iron clothes).
- You will always have a copy of the lecture for later reference.

2. Disadvantages

Here are some of the disadvantages of learning from audiotapes and videotapes:

- Without a set time and place, like a live class, you may lack the self-discipline to watch/listen at a proper pace. Many people tend to cover the material on tape all at once as the deadline for the course looms.

- The ease with which the taped class can be interrupted means that you may be too tolerant of interruptions and, therefore, fragment your learning too much.

- You may lack the self-discipline to be properly active and working during the taped lecture. It may be too tempting to be passive. After all, you can't miss anything because you can just replay the tape.

- You can't ask questions of the instructor immediately. Most distance learning formats do allow for telephone, fax, or e-mail contact with instructors, but only at predetermined times. You lose the spontaneous question-and-answer environment that is part of the live classroom experience.

- You are not part of a group. You have all the material from a lecture or seminar, but you have no interaction with other classmates. Sometimes the questions and comments of your peers are just as informative and stimulating as the lecture presentation.

3. Learning strategies

If you do choose to learn from audiotapes or videotapes, here are some guidelines to follow:

- Treat each learning session with taped material as if it were a live class. Do all the techniques and note-making strategies outlined in this chapter. Remember, note making is a learning activity, not just a recording function.

- Develop the attitude of "do it right the first time." The passive approach is a waste of your valuable time. If you don't have the time or energy to be active and make notes properly the first time, when will you find time to sit through the entire lecture again? You should be spending that time on other learning activities, such as review, note enhancement, and rehearsal.

- Listen/watch taped material while doing something else only *in addition* to a proper learning session. As we know from the discussion of memory and concentration, doing another activity while you are trying to concentrate in a learning situation will interfere with the quality of that learning. Therefore, if you listen to your audiotapes while jogging, and that is your only time to listen, you are shortchanging yourself.

12.

Study tools

The purposes of this chapter are to reinforce the notion of using the techniques outlined in other chapters as study "tools," and to provide more detail about two of the most useful "power tools." You should think of individual skills, hints, and techniques as components of your well-stocked toolbox of learning.

a. Basic tools: The essentials

The essentials of learning are the primary tools in your toolbox. They are listed here in order of importance and in the order in which you should devote your time to them.

1. Reading and making reading notes

Few of the other study tools described in this book will be very useful to you unless you spend time mastering basic study reading technique and learning to make effective notes from your reading. Review chapter 10 on study reading. This is your most important tool.

2. Listening and making lecture notes

The second most important tools are those you develop to get the most out of your classes and lectures — listening to a lecture and making notes. Review chapter 11 on making notes.

Each is given a bag of tools,

A shapeless mass and a
*   book of rules;*

And each must make,
*   ere life is flown,*

A stumbling block or a
*   stepping stone.*

R. L. Sharpe

3. Sleep

It may surprise you that sleep is included as a study tool and that it is ranked so high. A brain that is consistently deprived of sufficient sleep will never work properly. It's like having a rechargeable drill that you never let get fully recharged. It won't ever work to its full capability. However, it's amazing how much work you can get out of it if you replenish the power supply. Sleep is how you replenish your brain's power.

Not only is sleep essential to good mental and physical health, but it is a key component to shifting information from short-term memory into long-term memory. Sleeping does not mean your brain is completely inactive. Some areas are being restored through rest, but other kinds of activity are also going on. Studies show that material learned or reviewed just prior to sleep is the most efficiently stored and most easily recalled. Use this power to organize your study sessions. Review important material before you sleep — and make sure you are getting enough of that sleep!

4. Use your pen . . . or pencil . . . or crayon

Develop the habit of writing, rewriting, and rewriting again. It is the activity most like what you will have to do in an exam, yet it is the least practiced of output activity. Why? Because it takes effort. But the rewards surpass the effort expended.

Draw pictures, doodles, geometric designs — whatever seems to your mind to fit the subject. The best form of drawing for study purposes is mind maps (see section **b.2.** below).

5. Use your voice

An excellent output activity tool you must develop is your voice. Rehearse out loud. Repeat key points in many different intonations, inflections, and accents.

Give a speech or lecture as you teach the material to another (very understanding and patient) person.

Use rhyme. Try singing. Make the material into new lyrics for a tune that you already know and cannot forget, such as "Happy Birthday," "Twinkle Twinkle Little Star," or the national anthem. You will never think of "O Canada" or the "Star Spangled Banner" the same way again if you use the music to memorize the process of photosynthesis.

Men, in teaching others,

learn themselves.

Seneca

6.   Mnemonic devices

Mnemonics is the general name given to anything that assists your memory. Review all of chapter 5, which covers memory, and use those principles to create mnemonic devices that will help you remember lists and sequences.

The next section gives you some ideas on where you should record your mnemonic devices so you practice them and can refer to them easily.

b. Power tools

Once you are well on your way to mastering the basic tools, you can begin to add some power tools to your toolbox. The two best power tools you can use in your studying are flash cards and mind maps. These are truly two of the master keys to studying smarter, not harder.

1. Flash cards

Sometimes the simple things are the most effective. The first power tool you should add to your toolbox of learning skills is the frequent use of the simple flash card.

Use these cards for efficient studying during the fractions of time in your day that are usually wasted: waiting for the bus, shaving, eating your breakfast, waiting in line at a bank, etc. They also make good self-testing devices if you use the front and back. Make your own — don't buy them. The act of making them and the mental decision-making involved beforehand is a very valuable learning activity.

Sample #3 shows some examples of the kind of information you can put on flash cards. First, you can simply make a compact list that is portable, readable, and can be rehearsed anywhere, such as the list of Saxon kings of England or secretaries general of the United Nations.

Flash cards are particularly useful in learning and reviewing many different aspects of languages. Using German as an example, you can test yourself in basic vocabulary by putting the German word on one side and then the English meaning on the back, along with any other relevant information, such as the case of the noun.

Intelligence . . . is the faculty of making artificial objects, especially tools to make tools.

Henri Bergson

Man is a tool-using animal. Without tools he is nothing, with tools he is all.

Thomas Carlyle

Secretaries General of the U. N.

1. Trygve Lie	Norway	1946 - 1953
2. Dag Hammerskjöld	Sweden	1953 - 1961
3. U Thant	Burma	1961 (acting)
		1962 - 1972
4. Kurt Waldheim	Austria	1972 - 1981
5. Javier Pérez de Cuéllar	Peru	1982 - 1991
6. Boutros Boutros-Ghali	Egypt	1992 -

Saxon Kings of England

		Edred	946-955
Egbert	828-839	Edwy the Fair	955-959
Ethelwulf	839-858	Edgar the	
Ethelbald	858-860	Peaceful	959-975
Ethelbert	860-866	Edward the	
Ethelred I	866-871	Martyr	975-978
Alfred (the Great)	871-899	Ethelred II	
Edward the Elder	899-924	(the Unready)	978-1016
Athelstan	924-959		
Edmund I	939-946	Edmund II (Ironside)	1016

front

Geist

masculine noun

spirit or ghost

back

You can also use the cards to help you memorize tables of grammatical information, such as the declension of definite articles or the conjugation of verbs.

Flash cards can also be used very well as a place to record your mnemonic devices. For example, if you are using a unique sentence to help you memorize the eight bones of the wrist (e.g., Have two nasty trolls take lovely people cycling), write the sentence on one side of the card and the key on the other side:

Have	Hamate
Two	Trapezium
Nasty	Navicular
Trolls	Trapezoid
Take	Triquetrum
Lovely	Lunate
People	Pisiform
Cycling	Capitate

There are dozens of other possibilities. Simple, yet very powerful, flash cards can become a major part of your study routine.

2. Mind maps: The best study power tool ever invented

The basic notion of mind maps has been around for a long time. However, it wasn't until the 1974 publication of Tony Buzan's *Use Your Head* that a formalized learning tool and system based on the use of mind maps was introduced.

To become the ultimate power user of mind maps, I highly recommend that you purchase a copy of Buzan's 21st-anniversary edition of the original book, *The Mind Map Book*. It is well worth the expense and the time it takes to go through it very carefully. Mind maps are truly the best study power tool ever invented.

(a) What is a mind map?

To put it simply, a mind map is a drawing — a graphic representation of the material you want to learn and the relationship its parts have to an overall picture (and to each other). There is a lot of complex theory behind the proper use of mind maps, but they are essentially just drawings, usually with textual labels and inserts, that just happen to have a remarkable capacity for enhancing learning. They are literally a map of the material to be learned.

(b) Basic principles

Begin your drawing in the middle with the overall concept and work your way out. Add progressively smaller levels of detail as your map radiates out from the central image.

Summarized below are Buzan's six basic "laws" that he says are essential to creating true mind maps and not just cluster drawings.

Use emphasis. Find as many ways as you can to create visual emphasis in your mind maps. Use some or all of the following:

- Colors
- Drawings (pictures, 3-D boxes, spheres)
- Different spacing
- Borders around words
- Various kinds of lettering

Use associations. Use techniques to connect things together visually:

- Arrows
- Branches
- Color coding
- Train tracks
- Rivers

Be clear. Neatness isn't essential, but clarity is! Use these guidelines to avoid creating confusion in your mind maps:

- Use printing rather than cursive script.
- Use as few words as possible on a line (preferably only one).
- Make lines related to central ideas thicker than other lines.
- Keep images and drawings clear.
- Try to keep words reading horizontally if possible.
- Make the lines long enough so your words fit on them.

Develop a personal style. Do not be afraid to create your own personal style. One of the major reasons

Journey over all the universe in a map . . .

Cervantes

this technique works so well is because it is a reflection of the uniqueness of the creator's mind. Buzan emphasizes this in his writings and it is a vital part of success with mind maps. Your initial attempts will mostly be mimicking examples you see. You won't experience the true power until you try your own ideas for organizing the information. Let your imagination be your guide. Even break a few of the "laws" listed here if you think the result will be a mind map you can use more effectively.

Use hierarchies. This is essentially a reminder that you start with the main concept in the middle of your map and have the branches radiate out in descending order of detail and importance.

Use numerical order. If some sort of numerical sequence is essential to the material you are mapping (like a chronology or an order of actions), make certain you number the items in your map. You can even draw colored arrows to help remind you of the prescribed sequence.

(c) Stages and examples

You can use mind maps to summarize ideas, essays, movies, novels, chapters, books, or entire courses. The more practice you get using this tool, the more possibilities you will see.

Sample #4 shows a mind map created from some material you all should be familiar with by now — the information in chapter 3 about the brain. Using a very simple approach, Sample #4 shows how a mind map develops.

The mind map begins with a core idea (Sample #4, Stage 1). Then the main topics are added as "trunks" that grow out of the main theme (Sample #4, Stage 2). Notice that there are different ways you can draw this connection. You should use whatever forms seem to you to best fit the material.

The next level of detail is added as "branches" off these larger trunks (Sample #4, Stage 3). Yet another level of detail is then added with more branching (Sample #4, Stage 4). Remember, if you are generating lists, try to make it clear that they are equal under the heading — such as the three different brains that branch off from the triune brain.

Stage 1

Stage 2

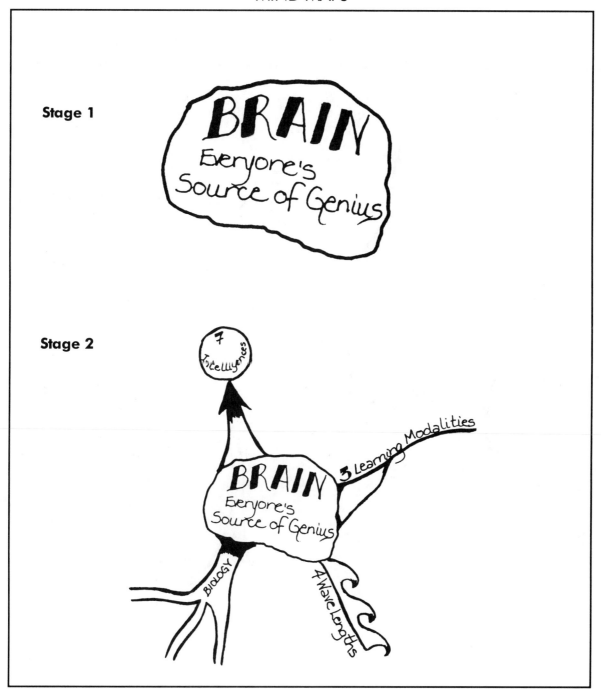

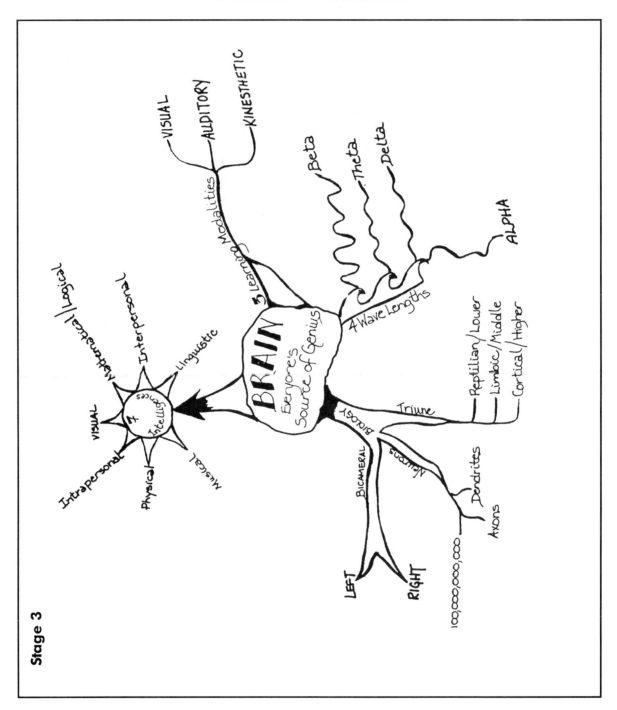

Stage 3

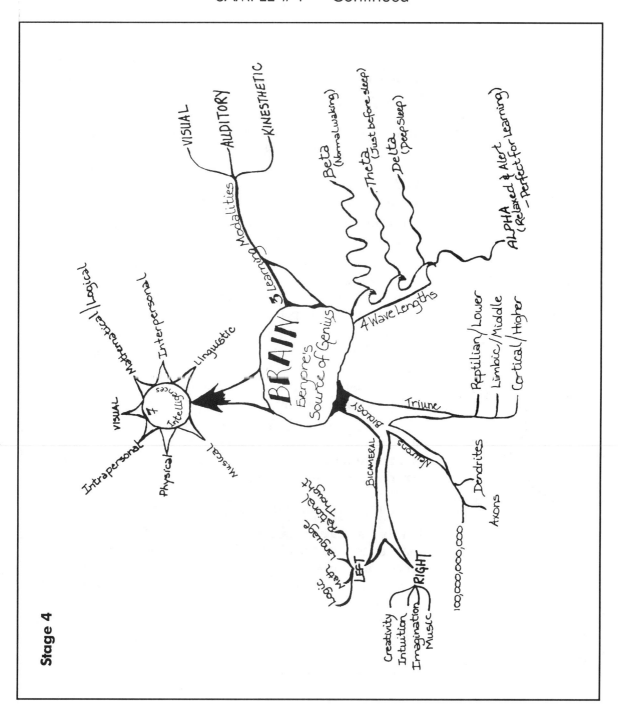

Stage 4

Sample #4 shows a pretty rudimentary mind map. There isn't any color and the organization is simple, but it resembles what yours should look like in your initial attempts.

If you want to see some amazing examples of what an experienced mind mapper can do with a little imagination and some color, take a look at Buzan's *The Mind Map Book.* You may get inspired by what you see.

(d) How to use mind maps in your studying

Mind maps should be a major output activity. An effective sequence of study tool use is to have good reading and listening skills as your primary tools, proper note-making skills from reading and lectures as your secondary tools, and mind-map making as your first tertiary level tool.

Use the mind maps as a way of testing yourself on recall and understanding the relationships between elements of the topic.

Use mind maps as a note-making device by itself. It may seem awkward at first, but you will find that mind maps are remarkably effective in organizing a lot of detail and recording that detail in a compact space.

See how many different kinds of mapping techniques you can use on the same information. You greatly enhance your learning activity if you make three different mind maps of a topic, rather than simply passively reading your written notes on that same topic three times.

Quickly reproduce your mind maps when you are writing an exam. It is especially helpful with essay exams when you want to recall as much detail as possible, as well as make sure you don't miss any major subtopics.

(e) Why do mind maps work so well?

One of the major reasons for the success of mind maps is that they reflect both the biological structure and the organizational tendencies of the brain. The static kind of organization that is typical of an essay outline (see chapter 14) is not as natural as the web of information graphically displayed in a mind map. A good mind map looks very much like a single neuron with many axons and dendrites radiating from its center and branching tentacles.

Mind maps also work so well because they employ many of your intelligences in their making, reviewing, and revising. You can use up to four or five of your intelligences making a mind map, compared to traditional note making, which uses only one or two.

c. Optional tools

Explore systems that make claims about enhancing your learning ability. Some of them have been touched on in this book and are well worth your attention. Some, such as most so-called "speed-reading" systems or memory courses, are a waste of time. But if you are a serious explorer, you will investigate them for yourself if you find them interesting enough — make your own decisions. You may find something of value that will improve your results.

Two "mastery" kinds of systems that merit deeper exploration are the "SuperLearning" and "Accelerated Learning" systems. These systems use the theories discussed in chapter 4 as more than just supplementary ideas. They base entire study patterns on the ideas of Dr. Lozanov and others in order to create programs that claim to improve your learning abilities to extraordinary levels. Much of this is still theoretical and experimental, but there have been some astounding results achieved in the areas of memory capacity and language learning.

A third system that merits more attention is Tony Buzan's "Radiant Thinking." It greatly expands on the basic principles that make mind maps so successful.

If you are interested in these systems, you can read the books mentioned in chapter 4 and this chapter. You can also get more details about specific programs by writing to the following offices:

SuperLearning
Ostrander & Associates
1290 W. 11th Avenue, Suite 105
Vancouver, BC V6H 1K5

Accelerated Learning Language Programs
Success Products
1725 South Hill Street
Oceanside, CA 92054

Buzan Centres
37 Waterloo Road
Bournemouth, Dorset, United Kingdom BH9 1BD

Form good habits.

They are as hard to

break as bad ones.

Unknown

Be careful with these optional tools. As intriguing and tantalizing as the results from these specialized programs may be, don't get carried away. Stick with fundamentals of good study techniques and attitude as outlined in this book. There is no quick fix to study problems or short cut to excellent grades, so do not get sidetracked by these kinds of esoteric programs. They are worthy of your investigation if you have mastered the basic tools and the best power tools, but not until you have achieved that mastery of the fundamental skills.

13.

Examinations

Examinations are to formal learning as races are to Olympic training. They are the final performance for which the participant must travel a long road of preparation. The exam, like the race, is only a small part of the story. There are many long hours, weeks, and months of serious training that must be undertaken before the examinee and competitor can even hope to be at his or her best on the fateful day.

It is impossible to compete as an Olympic athlete if you begin training only a week before the games. There is no "all-nighter" for the Olympian. It's the same for exam performance. Without the proper long-term work and study, you have no hope of optimum results. So, once again, you will read about the necessity of preparation — it is the key to the results you desire.

a. Examination preparation

Of all the stress-relief and coping techniques there are, the strategy that works best is to be as prepared as humanly possible. Nothing eliminates anxiety as well as knowing what to expect and being ready for it.

1. During your course

The best approach for good long-term preparation is to look at the entire year or semester as preexam studying. Because there is often a long time between the start of classes and the first major exam, students usually fail to make a strong link in their minds between regular studying and the frantic cramming that occurs in the days and hours before the exam itself. In fact, it's all exam studying, and you should work to develop that attitude.

(a) Know what is expected

As early as possible in the course, make sure you get a clear picture of what is expected of you. How many exams and tests will there be? How much is each worth? When will they be scheduled? Keep track of all your pending exams by writing them down on a calendar.

The date of each exam and its importance in the course is information you need to make plans and allocate your study time. It makes sense to spend more time on the exam you have two days from now that is worth 30% of your final grade and less on the quiz in another course that is worth only 5%. But you can't begin to make those kinds of vital decisions until you have a clear picture of what's expected of you in each course.

(b) Make a plan

Develop a plan for each course that will result in your covering all the material well before the exam is scheduled. You will not have time to do perfect preparation for every course — some decisions will have to be made. You are better off making a definite plan about your priorities and study timing rather than simply reacting to each looming exam as a crisis situation. Remember, if you don't plan to control your work, it will soon control you.

(c) Do the reading

Do the required reading for each course. Don't fall so far behind that you will be in danger of missing basic material. You must spend your preexam study time doing proper, effective study reading with active note making along the way. See chapter 10 for a review of study reading technique.

(d) Go to every class

Read chapter 11. Don't skip classes. Don't sit passively in your lectures waiting to be taught. Make a commitment to be an active learner in each and every class.

(e) Regularly review

Do the regular review of reading and lecture notes recommended in chapters 10 and 11. Like Olympic training, most of the work and preparation for your "event" has come in all the months and weeks beforehand. You can't expect to have command of your course work if you never look at it until a few days before the exam. Regular review throughout the school term is the key.

2. Immediately before the exam — the "homestretch"

In the week or few days immediately preceding the examination, you need to shift from the steady reading, note making, and review stage into an intensive study phase. Your goal during this period is to make your mind capable of peak-performance recall of all the relevant information required for the exam. You build on the solid preparation throughout the year or semester so far.

(a) Step 1: Gather all material

There is only a short time in which to review what you've learned and activate it for the exam. Take an extremely organized approach. The first step in that process is gathering together all the material you need to review: textbooks, lecture notes, reading notes, lab books, seminar handouts — everything.

(b) Step 2: Make a schedule

Create a schedule for the time between now and the exam. If you haven't used a schedule at all during the school year, now is the time to start. Within that schedule you must account for the following:

- The context of your other exams. You have to set priorities. For example, if you have another exam on the same day worth 60% of your final grade, and this one is worth only 15%, obviously you should spend more time on the other exam.

- Schedule enough time to ensure that you cover all the essential information and topics.

- Leave time aside in the hours before the exam to simply review and rehearse what you have already covered up to

Do every day or two something for no other reason than that you would rather not do it, so that when the hour of dire need draws nigh, it may find you not unnerved and untrained to stand the test.

William James

that point. If circumstances have compelled you to leave some holes in your preparation, you'll just have to live with it. The final hour or two before the exam is not the time to try to learn new material. It creates high anxiety and erodes the good preparation you may have done on other information. If you schedule review only for that last block of time, you are less likely to feel pressure to cram a new topic in there.

However, unless they actually plan for review time and commit to it, most people have a tendency to skip the review stage — especially if they are stressed out, preparing for an exam, and trying this approach for the first time. An actual plan makes it less likely that you will skip it because it is a reminder that it is important and "okay" to review — to go over old material to consolidate rather than to gloss over something you don't know very well.

- Pad your estimates. Give yourself more time than you think you'll need. Even though you should double or even triple your normal study time when an exam is looming, do not skimp on meals, sleep, and short breaks for exercise. But life will inevitably intervene and throw your schedule off. Try to allow for that in your planning.

(c) Step 3: 30-minute overview of material

Begin your actual studying with a quick review of everything in the course. This is meant to give you a general overview of the topics for which you are responsible and set you up for Step 4. It will give you a chance to remember some of the topics you haven't seen in a while (even the best regular reviewer will miss something). Spend no more than 30 minutes on this step. Think of it as a warm-up.

(d) Step 4: Create a menu of what you need to know

Next, you should create a fairly detailed listing of all significant information you will need to know for the exam. Completing this step will involve a more detailed skimming of your notes, texts, and other material. Write out each topic as you come across it in your quick review. Don't worry about organization yet. After you have compiled an exhaustive list you will evaluate its contents and add or delete items as you see fit. Finally, rewrite your list according to the best organizational pattern you think appropriate.

In general, this exercise should take one to three hours and result in a three- to six-page document, depending on the length of the course (these estimates are based on typical four- or eight-month courses at college and university). Writing a six-page outline may seem like a lot of work, but consider that you have reduced the pile of notes, books, and reports to a short, manageable document. That is quite a feat of synthesis.

This is a valuable learning exercise as well as an organizational one. Consider it a higher level of warm-up. You end up with a complete picture of what's ahead of you: a kind of menu, or table of contents, for the course and a road map through all the material.

Make three copies of your menu. The first copy becomes your to-do list for Step 5; the second copy for Step 6; the third copy for Step 7.

(e) Step 5: Intense review of material

Begin with the first topic on your list. Read all the material you have that is related to that topic. Read slowly, carefully, and attentively. As you do this for each item on copy 1 of your menu, cross it off the list.

(f) Step 6: Practice A LOT of output

After the initial intense review, 90% of the rest of your preparation time should be spent on output activities. These include, but are not limited to —

- teaching it to someone else,
- making flash cards and using them,
- mnemonic devices,
- mind maps,
- giving a speech,
- creating a song,
- other pictures or doodles, or
- writing.

All the various forms of active output practice are valuable. However, since the vast majority of your exams will be either written (essay or short answer), or require recall of material to be written (e.g., formulas for math or vocabulary in languages) or recognition of written words (e.g., multiple-choice or true / false), you should spend most of your time on flash cards and writing as your output activities.

(g) Step 7: Test yourself

The basic techniques of testing are to look away while reciting, or to write out what you know. These are verbal and written forms of output. Check back with the source and it becomes a simple test of your recall.

Go a step further and construct actual practice tests in the form you will be using during the exam. Make up your own multiple-choice questions. Try to devise problems based on material you think your instructor will likely cover on the exam. Construct your own essay questions and practice answering them in the same time you are likely to be given during the real exam.

If you have experienced difficulty in exam situations before, testing yourself is not only a good way to solidify the course content in your long-term memory, but you can also practice functioning in the artificial atmosphere of the exam room.

(h) Step 8: Keep going

Repeat Steps 5 to 7 until you feel you have almost *over learned* the material. Don't stop at a level at which you have just marginal recall of some vital information. Your goal is to know the material so well that you will be able to remember it under the pressure of the exam situation. That kind of pressure is difficult to simulate during your preparation. The best way to get ready is to rehearse and practice your output past the point you feel you need to for effective recall under the low-pressure situations outside of the exam room.

3. Practical details

You can also prepare yourself for the exam situation by anticipating the practical things that can go wrong and cause serious problems for your exam performance.

- Know the format of the exam (Is it one hour or three hours? Is it multiple-choice, essays, or problem-solving?)
- Be certain of the time and place of the exam. If it's scheduled to be in a room or building you are not familiar with, go for a visit in advance. It helps to visualize your success and easy handling of the situation if you can picture the

actual site. Find out where the nearest bathroom is to your exam site.

- Buy extra pens, pencils, batteries, and other items you will need to take with you. If you have medication that you may need, make sure you have an adequate supply.

- If you are getting a ride to the exam, or taking the bus, double-check the schedule and arrangements. Plan to arrive early. It's always a bad idea to arrive late or just in the nick of time but panting for breath. Planning to be at the exam site early also allows for something to go wrong and still gives you time to get there.

4. Anticipation as a study guide

Use your knowledge of the course, the material, the instructor, and review of past tests to anticipate the questions that will appear on this exam. If you expect the questions to be multiple-choice or true/false, practice answering those kinds of questions. Making your own practice questions will give you insight into the test construction process and assist your guessing if you don't know an answer (see section **b.3.** below for more on guessing).

Ask the instructor what will be on the exam. Most teachers are willing to give you some direction. If not, try brainstorming with other classmates.

5. Dealing with anxiety

Preparation of the course material is the best intervention strategy for anxiety. If the uncertainty of your performance on the test is making you anxious and nervous — *do something about it.* Study. The whole process and individual strategies discussed in section **a.** are designed to help you take control of the problem. Severe anxiety is a tell-tale symptom of the problem having control over you.

If you have difficulty settling down to serious studying each time you sit down to work, chances are you are not going through the proper preparation. Read

chapter 4 very carefully again. The principles and techniques described there are just as relevant for the "homestretch" as they are for the study sessions in the middle of the semester.

Preparation of your in-the-exam anxiety strategy is also a good idea if you are prone to stress problems during the exam. Be ready if it happens. Practice the relaxation and focus techniques that work best for you so they can be employed quickly if you have a panic attack during the test.

And remember, this is just a test of your recall of a body of knowledge on a specific day in a specific artificial format. This is not a test of your self-worth. While you should certainly take it seriously, no exam, no matter how important, is an indication of your value as a person.

Those who believe they can and those who believe they can't are both right.

Anonymous

b. Writing the exam: Tips for success

1. The day of the exam

The time just before the beginning of the exam can be crucial to how well you consolidate the information you have worked with, and how calm you remain. Here are some basic tips and strategies for what to do during this time:

- Get plenty of sleep the night before. At this point, an hour of sleep is more valuable to your performance than an hour of extra cramming.

- In the hours immediately before the exam, don't try to learn anything new. Use this time to review and rehearse what you already know. Practice output, don't read passively.

- Time and regulate your eating and drinking according to the principles set out in chapter 11. (Don't eat a heavy meal, don't drink alcohol, and don't use a lot of diuretics, such as coffee.)

- Arrive early.

- Use positive visualization and self-talk. Imagine yourself doing well, recalling easily, and calmly dealing with uncertainty and difficult questions.

- Review your anxiety strategies. If you're really ready, you probably won't get an anxiety attack, but at least you will be ready if you do.

- Find a seat where you will feel most comfortable (e.g., near heat if you tend to feel cold, or by a window for fresh air). Arrive early enough to get the seat you want.

- Generally, avoid talking to other nervous students. It will feed your anxiety and inhibit your concentration. Focus on the material and your certain feelings of mastery over it.

- Have all your materials ready (extra pens, pencils, calculator, extra batteries, and any other material you are allowed to bring in). Pack it all the night before and have it waiting for you by the door.

2. General principles for all exams

Strategies for specific kinds of exam structures are given in sections **3.** and **4.** below. There are, however, some principles that are valid for all forms of exams and exam situation.

- Stay for the whole exam. Even if you think you've done all you can, stay to the end. Relax, let your mind wander. You'll be surprised what comes back to you in a relaxed state that helps you improve answers or answer a question you were stuck on earlier. Give yourself that chance. Only make changes you are certain of.

- Ignore what others are doing, what questions they are working on, and when they are leaving. Focus on your own work and your own pacing.

- Read all directions carefully. The single biggest cause of error on exams is simply failure to read the instructions. If you are told to answer three of seven questions and you only do two, you will obviously lose a lot of marks. Take time on this small task.

- Read each question very, very carefully. Not reading a question properly results in many silly errors. Don't answer the question you think you see; answer the question that's really there.

- Budget your time wisely. Spend time on each question or section according to how much it counts toward the mark. If an essay counts for 25% of a two-hour exam, you should spend no more then half an hour on it. Stick to a strict allocation initially, then return to unfinished items if you have time left over.

. . . you can have no test which is not fanciful, save by trial.

Sophocles

- Do what you are confident of first. Don't do the questions in the exact order presented on the test unless specifically told to do so in the instructions. If you get stuck, move on and come back later. Let your brain work on the question for a while. Meanwhile, you can finish the easy questions and build your confidence. If you do questions out of order on paper separate from the exam sheets, make sure they are clearly marked for the examiner.

3. Objective tests (multiple-choice and true/false)

Multiple-choice and true/false exams are often called "objective" because there is a predetermined correct answer. They are also called "recognition" tests because the correct answer is somewhere in front of you — your task is to recognize it.

If the questions are constructed properly, there should be no debate about the correct answer; there should be no need for interpretation. But there are often very minor distinctions that make the difference between wrong, could be right, and definitely right. Here are some strategies for increasing your success with these kinds of exams.

(a) Multiple-choice strategies

The main part of a multiple-choice question is usually referred to as the *stem*. It is often in the form of a statement that is completed by one of the several alternatives offered below it. The question may also be in the form of a question to which you select an appropriate response from the choices given.

- Do the easy questions first. Skip the difficult ones and go back to them later. Plan to make three passes through the questions: first for the easy ones, second for those you have to think and work hard to answer, and a third time for those where your response will be more than 50% guesswork. Your goal is to make certain you answer all the easy ones first and get those marks. Getting stuck on hard ones early in the exam not only wastes time, but builds frustration that blocks the free flow of recall. The confidence building that occurs as you get several questions correct will relax you and help your recall for the more difficult questions later.

- Make sure you understand the stem and each of the possible alternatives. Do not make a rushed response.

- Immediately rule out the obvious wrong and foolish alternatives. These will be obvious more often than you might think. It is difficult to concoct several wrong choices that will have the appearance of being right. Sometimes test makers get lazy or fatigued and many alternatives will be of poor quality and easily spotted.

- Choose the answer that is *most* correct. There may be choices that seem very similar or also correct. In such a situation it can be deadly to simply select the first plausible alternative without reading all choices.

- Work actively. Circle and underline key words, tenses, plurals, etc.

- Check for inconsistency in number agreement. If the stem is singular, but one of the alternatives is plural, it can likely be eliminated.

- Check for verb tense agreement. If the stem is written in the present tense and an alternative is in past or future tense, it can likely be eliminated.

- Check for other grammatical incongruities between the stem and the alternatives. There may be clues to help eliminate alternatives.

- On the second and third passes, let yourself doodle and brainstorm on a piece of scrap paper. This can often stimulate other intelligences to help you recall information.

- Visualize yourself studying this material. You'll be amazed how often you can actually "see" the answer on the textbook page or in your notes.

Should you ever change your answers? That is always a difficult decision. Always trust your instincts — you are most likely to be right with your first choice. Only change an answer if you can convince yourself that your initial choice is definitely wrong and you are confident of an alternative.

And what about guessing? Here are some hints to take advantage of lazy or otherwise faulty test construction (these are not always true, only hints about what is likely):

- If one answer is substantially longer, it could be the right answer.

- If there are two exact opposites, the answer could be one of the two.

- Since it is psychologically easier to write true statements than several false ones, a choice that says "all of the above" is more likely to be right, while "none of the above" is more likely to be wrong.

(b) True/false strategies

For true/false exams, use many of the same strategies as for multiple-choice exams. In many ways, true/false exams are like multiple-choice, but with only two alternatives. Many of the same approaches and test construction errors apply.

- Do the easy questions first. Don't leave sure points behind if you run out of time.

- Be careful of guessing. Some exams are set up so that there is a severe penalty for incorrect guessing and wrong answers are subtracted from right. In this situation, guessing can seriously reduce your score. If there is no penalty, guess away! You have a 50% chance of getting it right.

If it comes down to guessing, there are structural cues that are peculiar to true/false exams:

- Statements that are ardent and use definitive words, such as "always," "never," "all," "must," "every time," and "none," are usually false.

- Statements that use less absolutist language, such as "usually," "most often," "likely," "probably," "could," "might," "should," and "rarely," are usually true.

- Since it is easier to write true statements than to create plausible false ones, longer statements are more likely to be true than false, and true is the best last-ditch guess.

4. Essay exams

The purpose of essay questions is to test your ability to think clearly and quickly, to organize relevant information, and to present that information in a coherent manner. Although it may seem to students that this kind of test is a medieval form of torture, it is actually one of the best methods of determining which material students really know and if they understand its significance. Essay exams are much more difficult to mark, so most instructors do not create this type of question for the thrill of grading them. Remember, you are writing only one essay, but the examiner will be reading and grading many. Keep that in mind as you write. You should make it easy for the reader to read and understand your essay; don't make it harder on the reader than you have to.

- Take time to plan and outline your answer. Use a minimum of 10% of the time available for each essay question for this purpose. For example, if you have 30 minutes, use at least 3 minutes for planning. Brainstorm as much material as possible to include in your answer. However, don't get carried away with this stage and leave too little time for actually writing the essay.

- If you have more than one essay question, do the brainstorming and outlining for all the questions before beginning to write.

- When writing, get to the point immediately — do not waste words. It is a myth that you can baffle instructors with bafflegab if you don't have anything else to write. Forget it! It becomes very obvious, very quickly, that you have little to say, and padding with irrelevant material will only irritate the marker. Nevertheless, if you have a lot of material that is relevant, or even tangentially so, write it down. Remember, there is a big difference between trying to mask your ignorance and demonstrating how much you know. If the relevance of the material is a stretch, leave it out if you already have plenty. If you're short of good material, then add the fringe stuff — but not too much.

- If the connection of your material to the question isn't obvious, explain the connection to the reader. This gives you an opportunity to demonstrate your understanding, as well as your recall of facts.

- Make sure you address the question being asked. Read it carefully and pay attention to the action words (e.g., "compare," "contrast," "discuss," "describe," "define," "state the pros and cons," "differences," "significance," "criticize," "outline," "summarize," "justify," "interpret," "prove").

- Pay attention to special instructions. (Are you asked to give examples? Are you asked to explain in the context of certain principles or facts?) Make sure you don't forget to tailor your material to carry out these instructions.

- Always attempt every essay question — never leave them blank. They usually count for more marks than any other type of question, and if you have done adequate preparation, there is always something you can write about the subject. It may not be a complete or fabulous answer, but always give yourself the chance to show what you do know. If it's blank, the marker must assume you know nothing about that subject, which is probably not true.

- If you run out of time, list the rest of what you planned to write in outline or point form. Let the marker know what you had planned to include in your answer.

5. Combination exams

If there is a mix of objective and essay questions, go to the essay questions first. Select a topic, outline it, brainstorm material, then leave that question. Answer other sections, but keep coming back to your outline as more ideas come to you. Use the rest of the exam to trigger ideas. Use time to relax and let a lot of ideas flow to the top to use in your essay questions.

6. Dealing with anxiety during the exam

The very best way to forestall a bout of extreme anxiety during the exam itself is to be extremely well prepared. The harder you work at the output activities and testing yourself, the stronger your confidence will be. You will have proven to yourself several times that you know the material and can recall it when needed.

Doubts, worries, trepidation, and uncertainty are all normal feelings before any type of performance. There is nothing wrong with having this level of anxiety, and it is unlikely to inhibit your best results. In fact, a reasonable level of fear heightens awareness and reaction time. However, as you read in chapter 3, extreme levels of fear and panic will block access to higher brain function.

If you have been subject to such debilitating panic attacks in the middle of an exam — blanking out or you can't stop shaking — prepare and practice two or three of the calm-inducing breathing and visualization techniques described in chapter 4. If you have done the work and practiced the output, a little 30- to 60-second relaxation exercise during the exam will help you get access to what's already there, waiting to be used.

When we quiet the mind, the symphony begins.

Anonymous

14.

Essays

This chapter is about strategies to help you get started, get organized, and finish your essay on time. This is not a chapter about learning to write. For that kind of instruction you should take a writing course, buy a book about writing, or get yourself a tutor or coach.

If you want to improve the quality of your prose, all the courses and books will come down to three essential activities:

(a) Read a lot of good writing.

(b) Think actively. Challenge your mind with new ideas.

(c) Write! Just do it, and do a lot of it. Practice the skill you want to develop.

a. What is an essay?

What is the purpose of the essay? What is the instructor looking for when you hand in the completed work? The answers will vary greatly between teachers, but their answers will all have the same core elements.

An essay is an extensive, independent creative project. The final product will show the level to which you can devise a focused point of view, marshal evidence to defend that argument, organize it coherently, and present it in clear expository prose. There, isn't that simple?

With all these elements, the essay is a marvelous testing arena. It tests your reading and thinking ability. It tests how well you can organize information and yourself. It tests your character by forcing you to do work in depth in a sustained fashion with a focus on a substantial objective. The instructor gets to see many facets of your academic ability. You get to learn a great deal about your subject and yourself.

Essay: A loose sally of the mind; an irregular indigested piece; not a regular and orderly composition.

Samuel Johnson

b. Three secrets to success with essays

1. Start early

The biggest mistake in essay writing has nothing to do with poor writing skills or improper research. It is starting the project too late to do a proper job. As you will see in section **c.** below, producing a final product you can be proud of involves many stages. If you follow that plan and give yourself adequate time for each step, you are almost guaranteed of writing the best essay you are capable of.

Don't ruin your chances of a good grade and a terrific learning experience by making the whole thing an exercise in crisis management.

It's easy to fall into the trap of procrastinating about the essay. Such a big job is daunting, and it's difficult to know where to begin. Also, the deadline is usually several weeks — maybe even several months — away, so there is no sense of urgency to make it a priority.

Make it your #1 Essay Writing Rule to always start the day it is assigned. This is your unbreakable rule — even if you learn of the essay on the first day of classes and it isn't due until the last day. Start work NOW!

2. Divide and conquer

The essay is the ultimate divide-and-conquer application. The prospect of completing a 10- or 20-page paper is intimidating. You know the teacher is expecting a brilliant argument, supported by plenty of evidence, expressed in superbly organized paragraphs. There's no doubt about it, it's a scary proposition.

The solution is to chop the big job into a series of smaller tasks that are easy to start, manageable, and relevant to the final goal (see Principle 7 in chapter 7). Section **c.** below gives you the basic stages of essay writing, but you should feel free to break each stage into as many smaller pieces as you need.

3. Time for rewriting

Always provide for enough time to edit and revise. The best strategy is to write a first draft as quickly as you can. Put that first draft away for a few days, then begin the hard work of rewriting. Make sure you plan your time to accommodate this approach. It can dramatically improve your final grade and is the most forgotten secret of getting great grades on essays.

c. Stages of essay construction

1. Stage 1: Be clear about the assignment

Be certain you understand the basic parameters of the project. When is it due? How long is it supposed to be (number of words or pages)? What are the possible topics? Is there any flexibility in changing topics? Do you have room to "reinterpret" the topic? What are the rules regarding late papers and extensions?

2. Stage 2: Focus your topic

This is what is commonly known as creating your thesis statement. Some beginning essay writers have difficulty with this concept and, as a result, have great difficulty developing a focused essay. This does take some practice, but it is like riding a bicycle: once you have the knack of it, it's something that never leaves you. In the beginning, the best approach is to shape your thesis by a gradual narrowing process. Eventually, you will skip many of the intermediate steps or do them very quickly.

Start with a general topic.

Shakespeare

You're not likely to cover that subject in 10 to 20 pages. You need to narrow the scope. Take one aspect of Shakespeare.

The plays of Shakespeare

That's still not very specific. Try limiting to one set of his plays.

The historical plays of Shakespeare

> Now you're getting there, but it's still too broad.
> Which of the historical plays will you deal with?

The "Henry" cycle of Henry IV Part I, Henry IV Part II, and Henry V.

> Okay, that could be manageable. What about the Henry cycle?

The three historical plays, Henry IV Part I, Henry IV Part II, and Henry V are not really "historical." They are more reflective of the politics of Shakespeare's time than of the time in which they are set.

> There are still several directions you can take the essay with such a topic sentence. You can make that your main argument and then the purpose of your essay is to prove it with evidence. Or you can take the statement as a starting point, but have the focus of your paper be a discussion of why Shakespeare wrote the plays this way. Was it by design, or did it happen unconsciously?
>
> You can develop your argument even further by asking "so what" questions about your thesis statement.

This makes Shakespeare unreliable as an historical source.

or

This gives us a wealth of "disguised" insight into the political ideas and sensibility of Shakespeare's time.

> Remember, the keys to focusing your topic are to keep narrowing the subject by reducing its scope (e.g., from all the plays of Shakespeare down to three of his historical plays), and asking questions that can develop an argument (e.g., "What about it?" "What is the significance of that?" or "So what?").

3. Stage 3: Brainstorm

At this stage your goal is to do some general reading, if necessary, and then generate some ideas. Plan on at least two brainstorming sessions. Take a block of at least half an hour and write down everything you can think of about your thesis statement. Don't edit yourself.

You can sometimes discover that you need to return to Stage 2 for further refinement.

4. Stage 4: Gather information — research

Research and gather information. Learn to use the new kinds of search facilities, such as computerized catalogues in many libraries and Internet access to many other libraries around the world.

Know when to stop. If your original assignment tells you how many sources to use, heed that instruction. Don't go overboard. If you are unsure if you have collected enough evidence for the size of essay you're doing, ask your instructor. Always do some research before asking, though. Teachers are more inclined to be helpful if they know you have already tried to do the work and find an answer for yourself.

Some essays in literature courses will prohibit the use of secondary sources. This means all your research will focus on your own interpretation of the poem, play, or novel under consideration. Don't try to fool instructors by passing off someone else's ideas as your own — they'll know.

If you find you have several books, papers, and chapters to read in order to assess whether they will be useful to you, use the preview / survey reading technique discussed in chapter 10. It will help you discover very quickly if the work will be helpful. If it is, you can still use the technique to glean the most information in the shortest amount of time.

Make notes as you go along. It is vital to document your sources and give full credit for the ideas of others. The best way to make sure you don't inadvertently plagiarize another's work is to keep detailed notes about where you find all your material. Record all details about the work: its author, exact title, publishing data, and page number.

Don't forget to make notes about your own ideas as well. The further you get into your research, the more you will find your own brain synthesizing what you are reading and generating its own interpretations, conclusions, and connections. Keep records of this just as diligently as if they were from a published book.

The format of your notes will depend on your preferred style. You can organize them on large legal pads or small recipe cards. Whichever pattern you decide to follow, remember to *do it right the first time.* Take down all the relevant source information, get the complete quotes accurately recorded, and don't forget to write legibly. Think of the time you'll waste if you have to find all this information a second time just because you were lazy and sloppy the first time.

5. Stage 5: Organize your material — outline

Organize your material into an outline. Select information, facts, details, and quotes that are relevant to your topic, and discard the rest. Include your own thoughts and ideas.

"Relevance" is a key concept; be careful of the important difference between irrelevant and contradictory. Don't throw out stuff that is important: relevant, but goes against your position. Use it; deal with it; acknowledge the other side of the argument. It weakens your essay if you ignore strong opposition.

Write your outline in point form. Be as detailed as you can. Organize your material according to the basic structure of an ideal essay (see section **e.** below).

Spend a lot of time on this. It's worth the effort. A good guideline is to construct 1 page of outline for every 4 to 5 pages of finished essay. For example, if your final essay is supposed to be 20 pages, your outline should be 4 to 5 pages. Build it gradually. Start with 1 page that covers the introduction, main topics in the body, and the conclusion. Then add more detail by including subheadings and sub-subheadings, along with key evidence.

6. Stage 6: Write the first draft

Write the first draft fast. Don't worry about polished prose.

Keep to the outline. Use it as a road map (where have you heard this concept before?) to guide you along. It will also help keep you from procrastinating about this stage.

At this stage, the essay will be rough. Don't worry about it; expect it to be rough — it's part of the process.

7. Stage 7: Do nothing — let it sit

Put your essay aside for a while. This is one of the more difficult things to do in essay writing, but one of the most valuable. You are more likely to make objective changes if you allow yourself the distance of a few days.

8. Stage 8: Revise and edit

Revise and edit your essay. Do this stage very carefully. You will be tempted to dive right in and begin rewriting the poor passages. Be disciplined. Go through the entire first draft looking at structure and evidence only.

Be ruthless. Don't be afraid to reorganize material or take out whole sections. Word-processing programs make it easier to rearrange material and see how it reads in new formats.

9. Stage 9: Write the second draft

Now you are ready for the actual rewriting phase. Write more slowly and carefully this time. Consider your use of words and try to avoid overuse of jargon and big words. Vary your sentence structure. Use as much of your ideas and material as you can, but be economical with your words. Apply the old writing cliché: if in doubt, leave it out.

10. Stage 10: Polish — the little things matter!

Spelling counts! There is no excuse for spelling errors with the proliferation of spell-checkers in word processors. But be careful with spell-checkers: the dictionaries have very limited capacity and may not contain much of the specialized academic vocabulary; you will still need to use a real dictionary for many words. Use the spell-checker as a starting point and a cue to remind you that spelling is important.

Make sure you use the format specified by the instructor (e.g., margins and titles). Also, be certain to use proper documentary format (e.g., footnotes and bibliography). If a certain format is specified in the assignment, use it and no other. You will lose marks if you use a different format for references just because you don't like the one required.

d. What does an ideal essay look like?

1. Structure

To attain your goal of an essay that is cohesive and presents a well-reasoned argument supported by evidence, you must consider the structure of the piece very carefully. You can't just throw all your facts and research together in a lump and hope the sheer weight of material will impress your instructor. It must be organized in a very particular pattern.

There is a beginning, a middle, and an end. That much should be obvious. But each of these large elements has a specific purpose and is the proper place for the various ideas and facts you have compiled. Here is a basic description of each part of your ideal essay.

(a) Introduction

The introduction will include a broad introductory statement of the subject, an early statement of the thesis, and some indication of your direction by summarizing the various topics you will touch on in support of your thesis. Your reader relies on this part of the essay to anticipate what will come in the main body. It is also the primary "hook" on which the reader will hang the evidence you present.

Everything that follows must be relevant to the thesis you have developed. Imagine how irritated you would be if a chapter in your textbook started discussing things that are only peripherally related to the topic of the chapter, or worse, were completely unrelated. They might be interesting divergences, but they have no place in that chapter. If that would make you mad, think about how the reader of your essay will react. You do not want to antagonize the person reading your essay.

(b) Body

The main body of your essay will be the longest section, taking up 85% to 90% of the writing. This is where you do the paragraph-by-paragraph development of each point that supports your thesis. In a 10- to 20-page paper, there would be no more than five to eight main points to make.

It is usually best to arrange your material so you build up to the most important point at the end. Although you should tailor the structure to the topic and instructor's requirements, a good general arrangement is to construct a lineup that is much like a good swimming relay: the second strongest goes first, the strongest goes last, and you fill in the middle in ascending order of strength.

(c) Conclusion

The concluding portion of your essay is where you restate your thesis and summarize the evidence you have presented. It is also where you have the most freedom to express your own opinions. Engage in a discussion about the implications of your thesis and what the ramifications and significance might be. Answer the question "So what?" and you will add a personal touch to the essay and demonstrate some creativity and independent thinking to the marker.

2. Writing style

Write in a straightforward style using clear, concise language. The worst of academic writing is opaque phrases full of meaningless jargon. Unfortunately, the worst is also very common, so you will see a lot of it. Don't try to emulate this kind of writing.

If your ideas are clear and well-founded, your writing should reflect that. If the material is well organized and you have taken time to build a solid argument, you do not need to be very fancy with your exposition. You can still use the precise words that make the necessarily subtle distinctions in academic argument without making your writing unnecessarily complex.

The truly great scholars have always been the ones who could communicate complex ideas in elegant yet simple, understandable prose. Some, such as Carl Sagan, Stephen Jay Gould, Daniel J. Boorstin, and Harold Bloom, can even make their ideas into best-sellers. Theirs is an accessible style to which you should aspire.

15.

Success: How to keep it going once you get it

a. Don't be content with "good enough"

Success is a habit. Failure and mediocrity are also habits. Which habit do you prefer to dominate your life?

That is not as dumb a question as you would first think. The world is filled with people who changed their old behaviors to achieve a short-term goal. Unfortunately, they returned to those old, bad behaviors after that goal was realized. Life slips back into the same mediocre ruts, and the gains made by the changed behavior disappear.

Is that what you want? Do you just want to learn enough study techniques to survive the next exam and then relapse into the poor study problems that caused the crisis in the first place? Or do you want to keep moving forward to becoming the wonderful life-long learner you really want to be?

It really is possible to unlock the genius that lies dormant inside you.

If you experience some success with the principles and strategies in this book, why not use that as a springboard to something even better? Don't be content with being average in your learning achievement. Average is as close to the bottom as it is to the top.

We first make our habits, and then our habits make us.

John Dryden

Oh! This learning, what a thing it is.

Shakespeare

b. Make a commitment to something better

The mind is a very powerful "answer engine." It will always find answers to questions we ask it. But you must be careful of which questions you ask. If you constantly ask yourself "Why do I fail?" or "What's wrong with me?" your mind will come up with answers.

However, if you ask different questions, such as "What will it take for me to succeed?" or "I wonder how good I can really get" or "What do I need to do to get an A in this course?" your mind will also generate answers for you.

If you make a commitment to searching for success and making habits out of the things that work for you, you'll be amazed at how many answers and solutions will seem to just appear in front of you. This isn't magic or power of positive thinking mumbo-jumbo. It is based on the way your brain and attention-focusing mechanism work.

All day long we are bombarded with sensory, emotional, and intellectual stimuli. It is impossible for all of it to register at a conscious level. Your mind will screen out 99% of what's out there. Your attitude, priorities, and focus will determine which 1% filters through to your awareness. Think about it.

For example, if you didn't care about golf, if it never entered your thinking throughout the day, you probably would not be aware of anything to do with golf. If, however, a friend dragged you out to play a round of golf one day and you got hooked on the game, you would think a whole new world had sprouted up in front of you. Suddenly you would notice all the golf courses in your town that you never noticed before and all the different golfing stores, golfing schools, driving ranges, and vacations related to golf. Golf was always there; you just didn't notice it because it wasn't part of what you told your brain to pay attention to.

The same pattern works for the outcome of your life. If you are convinced you are a failure and the world is against you, your mind will find plenty of evidence to support you, even if it has to twist the interpretation of some input. On the other hand, if you are committed to succeeding and are convinced the answer is out there somewhere, your mind will focus on finding that solution.

The thing always happens that you really believe in; and the belief in a thing makes it happen.

Frank Lloyd Wright

Now, it's not as simple as making a commitment and having the right focus. This will put the opportunities in front of you only. You have to commit to taking action when the answers are found.

c. Don't stay in one place

Don't become so content with where you are and what you know that you stop growing. Raise your standards for your life and yourself.

Once you achieve one goal or set of goals, devise new ones. Keep moving ahead. If you want to make the study tools in this book the beginning of a life of power learning and satisfying results in formal studying, turn to chapter 17 for a 10-Day Quick Start program.

d. Enjoy the journey

Let yourself enjoy the process of learning and improving your study capacity. Don't be afraid of failure, or rather, don't let fear of failure stop you from moving out of your comfort zone to try new ways of learning. Develop the attitude that success is never final, and failure never fatal.

e. *Kaizen*, consistency, and passion

If you really want the satisfaction and amazing opportunity that life-long learning can bring, then *kaizen*, consistency, and passion are the magic secrets to achieving. In fact, they are the secrets to all sustained success in life.

1. *Kaizen*

Kaizen is famous as one of the cornerstones of the success of Japanese industry. It is a principle that demands constant, incremental improvement every day. It comes from the attitude that is essential to successful warrior training in the martial arts. Success will not come all at once. Success comes if you commit to finding some small way to improve every day. It is the accumulation of these little steps that creates the biggest change. It is the consistent application of this principle that creates lasting change.

There is no quick fix to study problems. You may find a hint or tip that helps at the moment, but there will be no permanent

Even if you're on the right track, you'll get run over if you just sit there.

Will Rogers

change that is fast. A commitment to making small improvements in your study habits each day, each week, every month is what will make the difference.

2. Consistency

The thing you have to be consistent about is taking action. Each day, each learning opportunity that presents itself (or imposes itself, if you're taking a time-constrained course of study) has to be approached with the same attitude and skill set that will ensure success and maximum results.

Do the study smart techniques *all the time*, not just when you feel like it or think you have the time. Be consistent in what you do (if you're doing the right things), and success will follow almost automatically.

Success is not a sometime thing or occasional thing. Don't use the techniques in this book for emergencies only and then revert to your old habits. Use them consistently on every study task and you will have results you only dreamed of before.

3. Passion

Success becomes a habit that cascades on itself. It can become an upward spiral that seems to be propelled by its own momentum. Success with studying and learning is no different. It is a thrilling realization that you can learn anything, and even more thrilling to prove it to yourself over and over again.

Let success in learning excite you — not just about the exam or course in front of you, but about learning and study success for the rest of your life. Nurture a passion for learning, practice the techniques, and develop the study tools, and results will follow.

Think of it not just as a means to the end of getting a passing grade, but rather as an adventure — a wonderful exploration of your potential.

A consistent man believes in destiny, a capricious man in chance.

Benjamin Disraeli

The secret of success is constancy of purpose.

Benjamin Disraeli

f. Keep going

Go beyond the techniques and strategies in this book. Put your brain on a training course. Whether you are 18 or 80, your brain can improve and benefit from a program of strength training. Think of it as your genius muscle growth course. You can make incredible improvements if you develop the power tools outlined in this book. But think of what you could accomplish if you beef up the power source itself — your brain.

There are several books that are excellent starting points for such an endeavor. Here are four of the best to get you started:

- *de Bono's Think Course* by Edward de Bono (BBC Books, 1982, 1994)
- *Pumping Ions: Games and Exercises to Flex Your Mind* by Tom Wujec (Doubleday Canada, 1988, 1994)
- *Use Your Perfect Memory* (3rd edition) by Tony Buzan (Plume Books, 1991)
- *The Mind Map Book: Radiant Thinking, The Major Evolution in Human Thought* by Tony Buzan (BBC Books, 1995) (This is mentioned in chapter 12, but is worth reminding you of.)

Always bear in mind that your own resolution to success is more important than any other one thing.

Abraham Lincoln

Part IV

Specialty tools

16.

Top tips lists

This chapter offers summaries of the most important and inspiring facts, quotes, and ideas from the preceding chapters. Read them. Recite them. Remember them. Photocopy them and put them in your notebooks, on your wall, or give them to your friends.

Top 6 reasons to become a genius

1. The world is changing in favor of those who command knowledge.

2. Employability increasingly depends on the ability to learn fast and easily.

3. Almost all new industries — and their jobs — are based on information skills.

4. The competition for knowledge-based jobs will necessitate excellence in learning capability, not just adequacy.

5. Every career change will require upgrading of knowledge credentials and skills. Your learning ability must be kept honed and in peak condition.

6. Because you can. Such learning and intellectual level is within your reach. Try to achieve your maximum potential.

1. There are one hundred billion neurons in your thinking brain.

2. You have twenty thousand possible connections between each neuron.

3. There are more possible connections than particles in the known universe.

4. You have seven different, equal intelligences: linguistic, mathematical, musical, visual, physical, interpersonal, and intrapersonal.

5. The brain is really a triple brain: reptilian, limbic, and cortical.

6. Your brain is "two-sided": left for logical reasoning and analysis; right for creativity and intuition.

7. Alpha brain waves are the best type for studying — they create relaxed awareness.

8. You have three learning modalities: visual, auditory, and kinesthetic.

9. Neurons continue to develop and increase no matter what age the learner is.

10. You have the capacity to develop genius level results.

Top 10 facts about the brain

Top 10 characteristics of your study place

1. It is used only for studying — nothing else!

2. You have at least one back-up study place.

3. You have a comfortable chair you can sit in for hours.

4. It has a supply of clean air that is neither too hot nor too cold.

5. It has adequate, proper lighting.

6. You have it surrounded with positive images and items.

7. It is free of distractions from music and TV.

8. You have study places arranged at home and on campus.

9. It has enough space to spread out all your study materials.

10. It is enriched with other comforts such as plants.

It may seem silly, but positive affirmations work. Tell your mind what you want to believe, and eventually it will be perceived as the truth. Repetition makes positive affirmations "firm" in your mind. You are what you believe yourself to be. All attitudes are learned, so why not learn a positive attitude?

1. I can learn anything.

2. I learn easily.

3. I am a fabulous learner.

4. There is genius potential inside me. It will come alive.

5. I will perform at my best on this exam.

6. Everything will come back to me when I need it.

7. I am committed to being a consistently successful learner.

8. My brain is the most powerful bio-supercomputer in the universe.

9. Nothing can stop me.

10. I will continue until I succeed, no matter how many temporary failures might intervene.

Top 10 positive affirmations

Top 8 preparation techniques

1. Have a proper study place.

2. Have defined goals established for each study session.

3. Make sure each study activity fits your *real* priorities.

4. Have all your material ready at your desk before sitting down.

5. Prepare your state of mind with positive affirmations.

6. Prepare your state of mind with effective visualizations.

7. Prepare your state of mind with breathing exercises.

8. Prepare your state of mind with classical music.

1. Understand that study reading is slow and detailed. There is no speed reading in serious studying.

2. Build a road map of every chapter and book by surveying or previewing it.

3. Read the title and think.

4. Read the table of contents (if it's a book) or introductory paragraphs. Think about what to expect.

5. Read the conclusion.

6. Read any summary and review questions.

7. Read all major headings and subheadings.

8. Read the first sentence of each paragraph.

9. Examine all pictures and graphs carefully.

10. Before detailed reading, take the material from steps 3 to 9 and think. Activate all the knowledge you have gained from your survey.

Top 10 steps to effective study reading

Top 10

steps to

completing

an essay

1. Start early!

2. Give yourself enough time to do at least two drafts. Never hand in a first draft.

3. Divide and conquer. Follow a plan that divides the work into several manageable chunks or stages.

4. Set a time limit for each stage.

5. Always brainstorm your ideas before outlining or writing.

6. Always build a detailed outline before starting to write.

7. Write your first draft as quickly as you can. Let the polish come later.

8. Let the first draft sit for a few days before revising it.

9. Little things count. Check spelling and basic grammar.

10. Never hand the essay in late without prior approval.

1. Go to all classes. Don't skip any.

2. Don't eat a big meal or drink alcohol before class.

3. Review previous notes before class.

4. Be certain to do all required reading before each lecture.

5. Sit at the front.

6. Listen actively. Constantly question, conclude, and anticipate what the instructor is going to say.

7. Make notes in your own words. Use the instructor's exact words sparingly and only when essential.

8. Review notes immediately after class. Add as much material to your notes as you can remember.

9. Don't tape your lectures. It just postpones the real work. Do it right the first time.

Top 9 tips for effective note making

Top 10 exam preparation tips

1. Start preparation at the beginning of the course. Do the reading. Go to the classes.

2. Do regular review throughout the course.

3. Gather all your material together.

4. Make a schedule that ensures you cover all the major elements.

5. Do a quick 30-minute overview of the course.

6. Create a "menu" of all the material in the course.

7. Do one intense review of all the material with a detailed active reading of all notes and marked textbook passages.

8. Practice a lot of output activity. This is the secret to success in all exam preparation.

9. Test yourself frequently.

10. Prepare your best anxiety coping strategies.

1. Always know your priorities.

2. Set your plans to take action that achieves your priorities. This is the best defense against procrastination.

3. Do it right the first time.

4. Follow the principles of proper schedule making.

5. Use the power of to-do lists.

6. Keep track of all important dates and commitments on a calendar.

Top 6 aspects of good time management

Top 10 motivational quotes

1. Many of life's failures are those people who did not realize how close they were to success when they gave up. (Thomas Edison)

2. In the long run you hit only what you aim at. Therefore, though you should fail immediately, you had better aim at something high. (Henry David Thoreau)

3. First we form habits, then they form us. Conquer your bad habits, or they'll conquer you. (Dr. Robert Gilbert)

4. Most people don't plan to fail; they just fail to plan.

5. Never, never, never, never give up. (Sir Winston Churchill)

6. You see things that are and say "Why?" But I dream of things that never were and say, "Why not?" (George Bernard Shaw)

7. Destiny is not a matter of chance, it is a matter of choice; it is not a thing to be waited for, it is a thing to be achieved. (William Jennings Bryan)

8. Dost thou love Life? Then do not squander Time; for that's the stuff Life is made of. (Benjamin Franklin)

9. We first make our habits, and then our habits make us. (John Dryden)

10. The secret of success is constancy of purpose. (Benjamin Disraeli)

17.

10-day quick start program to supercharge your studying and keep it supercharged

a. How badly do you want to change?

The purpose of this book is not to provide you with some useful strategies for getting through the next exam just to have you relapse into the old habits that created the crisis in the first place. The true purpose of this book is to set you on the path of producing a meaningful, measurable change in the quality of your studying and learning.

The only way you are going to translate these new skills and techniques into consistently higher grades and long-term learning is to actually do the new things on a consistent basis. You must develop a pattern of behavior in which you consistently engage in activity that improves your learning. There are seven steps to creating this change.

Step 1

The first step in this change is knowing in the depths of your heart, soul, and mind that the behavior that got you in trouble is definitely not what is going to get you to the level you want to achieve. Believe that you have been on the wrong path and it's time to get off.

Step 2

Get a clear picture in your mind of the behavior and results you want for yourself. Use your senses and emotions to imagine exactly how you will feel when —

- you are able to remember everything you need to during an exam,
- you have complete control of your study time,
- you have a terrific set of study notes from your lectures and textbooks, or
- you get straight As!

Let yourself feel all the pride, exhilaration, and satisfaction that will result from your achievements.

Step 3

Devise a plan to overcome the inertia of getting started. Use the sample 10-day plan in this chapter to get you started (see section **b.** below). Then use it as a template to create your own program of never-ending study improvement.

Step 4

Take action! Begin the plan with the first step. Commit yourself to the full 10-day cycle. Start and don't stop.

Start today. Why not? Day 1 on the 10-Day Program will take only an hour or so. Why put it off? It's easy to get started.

Step 5

Keep track of what works and what needs to be adjusted. Don't expect to reach genius levels of results in the first 10 days. This is a cumulative process. Use what works and consolidate that behavior. Be honest with yourself about your weaknesses and don't avoid them in future 10-day programs.

Keep track of your progress, setbacks, and strategies. Create a learning journal to document your improvement.

Step 6

Go back to Step 1 and start a second 10-day cycle. Continue with the new behavior that comes easily. Improve it and make it the foundation of your new pattern of study success. Select one of the techniques or concepts that is difficult for you, and commit to practicing it for the next 10 days. Don't overload yourself, but also don't forget that real improvement comes at the expense of pushing yourself beyond your comfort zone.

Step 7

After 3 of the 10-day cycles, do a systematic review of your behavior and take an inventory of your new study skills. Then keep going.

Generate a new plan for the next 10 days based on the results you've recorded in Step 5.

b. The 10-day quick start program

The goal of this sample 10-day program is to give you a foundation in four of the most important fundamentals of good studying:

(a) **Belief in yourself** (discover the power of your brain).

(b) **Preparation** (prepare your study place and practice preparation techniques to get into the right state of mind for learning).

(c) **Discipline** (practice it by sticking to a 10-day program).

(d) **Activity**, not passivity (do the exercises each day; use your many intelligences).

Rules: If you miss a day, or do some tasks in a mediocre fashion, don't quit. Don't go back to the beginning. Forgive yourself, and start at the day you're on and go forward. One of the points of these first 10 days is to find where your strengths and weaknesses are. Find what you're good at, what you like doing, and make that your foundation. On that foundation you will build more skills from the things that didn't work out too well in the first 10-day cycle.

Don't expect to be perfect. Give an honest effort with the best focus you have at the time. Remember you will have more chances to get it right, but not so many that you can afford to waste time.

Trifles make perfection, and perfection is no trifle.

Micholangolo

Day 1 (a) Read chapters 1, 2, and 3.

(b) Let yourself get excited about the possibilities of being a supercharged learner.

(c) Do the following 30-minute writing exercise. Make two lists:

(i) Everything you have ever learned in your life.

(ii) Everything you would like to learn during the rest of your life.

The first list is to help point out just how good a learner you already are. The second list is to inspire you. You have the potential to learn anything on that list — maybe even everything if you have time.

Day 2 (a) Do everything from the list for Day 1 that you didn't get to do yesterday. Do not start today's work until you have finished what was assigned for yesterday.

(b) Read chapter 4 on preparation.

(c) Do the following 30-minute writing exercise: an analysis of your study place(s). Compare it with the elements of a good study place outlined in chapter 4. How does yours measure up? Make a list of any changes you need to make in your study place to improve it to an acceptable level.

Create a schedule so that you will make at least one of the necessary improvements on each of the remaining days of this 10-day program.

Day 3 (a) Do everything from the list for the previous days that you haven't done yet. Do not start today's work until you have finished what was assigned for those days. From now on, the first item for each day will be "catch up." It is your reminder to catch up on the previous assignments before doing new ones.

(b) Do the first item on your "study place improvement" schedule.

(c) Reread chapter 4 and make notes on the visualization and breathing techniques.

(d) Do a 30-minute relaxation exercise. Practice one of the visualization techniques for 15 minutes. Practice one of the breathing exercises for 15 minutes.

Day 4 (a) Catch up!

(b) Do the next item on your study place improvement schedule.

(c) Do a 30-minute relaxation exercise (choose techniques you haven't tried). Practice one of the visualization techniques for 15 minutes. Practice one of the breathing exercises for 15 minutes.

(d) Select a textbook that you will use for practicing proper study reading technique.

(e) Listen to some of the music recommended in chapter 4. Choose five pieces you will use as part of your preparation pattern.

Day 5 (a) Catch up!

(b) Do the next item on your study place improvement schedule.

(c) Read chapter 5 on memory.

(d) Practice a visualization and a breathing technique for ten minutes each. You should be getting good at these by now.

(e) Read chapter 10 on study reading.

Day 6 (a) Catch up!

(b) Do the next item on your study place improvement schedule.

(c) Read chapter 6 on concentration.

(d) Practice a visualization and a breathing technique for ten minutes each.

(e) Choose a chapter from the textbook you selected on Day 4. Read through it using the surveying/previewing technique in chapter 10. Make notes based only on the framework you get from this process.

Day 7 (a) Catch up!

(b) Do the next item on your study place improvement schedule.

(c) Read chapter 8 on goal setting.

(d) Practice a visualization and a breathing technique for ten minutes each.

(e) Read in detail the textbook chapter you surveyed on Day 6. Make notes using your own words. Underline and highlight only key words and phrases in the text itself. When you're finished, review the important points from the chapter. Rehearse these to yourself.

Day 8 (a) Catch up!

(b) Do the next item on your study place improvement schedule.

(c) Practice a visualization and a breathing technique for ten minutes each.

(d) Do some goal setting practice. Give yourself a mini-workshop by completing Exercise #5.

Part I

1. Begin with two sheets of paper. Write "Life" across the top of one and "Learning" above the other.

2. Divide each sheet into four columns. Write a heading at the top of each column: "4 to 6 months," "1 year," "5 years," and "10 years."

3. Now close your eyes and use some of the visualization techniques you have been practicing. Imagine what your life will be like at each of those benchmark times if you make no significant changes in your life in general and your learning/studying habits, specifically. What will your life be like at the end of four to six months (the usual length of a semester)? What about in a year? How about five years from now? Ten years? Let your imagination show you.

4. Take 15 minutes and write down what you imagined. Write quickly and vividly.

5. Do you like what you see? Will you be satisfied with that life? Can you see all your potential realized in that vision?

6. If you're not happy with the results of staying the same, go on to Part II. If you *are* happy with the results, go on to Part III.

**EXERCISE #5
GOAL SETTING**

EXERCISE #5 —
Continued

Part II

1. Begin with two fresh sheets of paper. Write "Life" across the top of one and "Learning" above the other.

2. Divide each sheet into the same four columns as before. Write a heading at the top of each column: "4 to 6 months," "1 year," "5 years," "10 years."

3. Now close your eyes and imagine what your life will be like at each of those benchmark times if you make many significant changes in your life in general and your learning/studying habits. Let your imagination run wild. Don't edit yourself. What would you like your life to be like? What kind of learner would you like to be? What could you accomplish if you could study at optimum capacity?

4. Take 15 minutes and write down what you imagined. Write quickly and vividly.

5. Do you like what you see now? Does it look different from what you produced in Part I? Will you be satisfied with that life? Can you see all your potential realized in that vision? How do you make this life with you as a supercharged learner become reality? Take Action! Start now!!

Now continue on to Part III.

Part III

1. Write down four to six actions that you can take today that will set you on the road to achieving your six-month or one-year goals. They don't have to be monumental, just do something. You have to practice taking action that is directly relevant to something you really want in life. Make two to three of your actions related to life in general, and two to three that are specifically tailored to improving your learning ability.

2. Make a commitment to do this every day.

Day 9 (a) Catch up!

(b) Do the next item on your study place improvement schedule.

(c) Practice a visualization and a breathing technique for ten minutes each. You should begin to feel very comfortable with this. By the time you begin your second 10-day cycle, you should feel that this is a natural part of how you start each study session.

(d) Write down two more actions you will take today that will keep you on the road to achieving your goals. Do them!

Day 10 (a) Catch up!

(b) Do the next item on your study place improvement schedule.

(c) Practice a visualization and a breathing technique for ten minutes each.

(d) Choose another chapter from your textbook and go through the entire study reading process, from survey through detailed reading to final review and rehearsal.

(e) Write down two more actions you will take today that will keep you on the road to achieving your goals. Do them!

(f) Make a promise to yourself that during the next 10-day program you will have no more than 2 days when you have any catch up to do.

18.

5-day emergency cramming guide

a. How bad is the situation?

You have been skipping most of the classes since the mid-term. It became too hard to get up for 8:30 a.m. lectures, and they were so boring anyway. The textbook wasn't much better. You have not read a word of it in over six weeks. There still seemed to be plenty of time to learn the material. It wouldn't be that hard. After all, you had slacked off before and still pulled it off in the end. Then, one morning you look at the calendar and are clobbered by the realization that all those weeks have melted away. There are only five days before the final exam. It would take a minimum of five *weeks* to make up for the wasted time. You're so far behind you can never catch up.

What are you going to do? It's time to make a decision. Will you panic? Will you spend the time in a depression and waste an opportunity? Will you give up and abandon the course?

You can never recover the time you have squandered. That is now beyond your control. But you can control how you will respond to the situation and how you will use the little time available. It is time to take action.

Assess the circumstances and be brutally honest with yourself. Will spending the next five days trying to salvage something from this course seriously compromise any other exams? Are the other courses in better shape than this one? If the five days are truly open for you to focus on the problem course, then you would be foolish not to take up the challenge and cram for the final. With a calm, systematic approach, there is still a chance you can create something positive from the situation. A grade of A is unlikely, and perhaps the best you can hope for is to pass. But don't throw away all the points available from a final exam. You might still fail this exam, but you could gain enough marks and impress the instructor with a few very good answers to earn a passing grade for the course as a whole. You never know.

You can use the situation as a learning experience. If you didn't believe enough in your potential and the ability of the principles in this book to help you make that potential come alive during the school term, then try them now. For five days, use the principles of smart studying. In such an intense, compressed time, there is still an opportunity to surprise yourself with your capacity to learn and perform on an exam. If you pass the exam — great for you. If not, you will at least have a head start on the next one (see Day 6 below).

b. Basic principles for effective cramming

You have a choice. You can waste the five days available to you, or you can use them effectively. If you choose the latter, there are several principles you must follow.

1. Prepare your mental attitude

You cannot cram effectively if you panic. Neither can you cram effectively if you have given up all hope.

Think positively. *Talk* positively. Use breathing and visualization techniques to feel positive (see chapter 4). This doesn't mean you should have impossible expectations. Be realistic about the possible outcomes, accept the inevitable consequences of having squandered so much study time, but don't give up all hope of getting something positive out of the situation.

Try to salvage something. Make sure the next five days are spent giving you the best possible chance to learn some aspects of the course well enough to answer exam questions.

Be calm. Be systematic. Envision a positive result. This is not self-delusion, but rather an attempt to make your mind receptive to what you're going to do in the next few days and make it more likely that you will remember enough to do well.

2. Make a plan that focuses on the possible

You can't do it all. Your goal must be to identify the essentials. Don't expect to learn everything you've neglected. Choose a subset of the course and commit yourself to learning that smaller body of material as well as possible in the five days you have.

This will be difficult to do. Your natural impulse will be to make some attempt to cover everything you should have done in the preceding weeks. You will need to be ruthless in order to have a chance at any success. Give up on some material so that you give yourself the opportunity to save some.

Use the principles of good exam preparation outlined in chapter 13 and set out a 5-day schedule to accomplish the best you can with what's left to you. Take each of the standard preparatory steps and compress them into the time available. Do not leave out any of the steps.

If you do not look at things on a large scale it will be difficult for you to master strategy.

Miyamoto Musashi

3. Follow the plan

Stick to your plan. Resist any temptation to stray from it or adjust. You simply don't have enough time to second guess yourself. Make a commitment, right now, that you will stay with your first decisions about schedule and priorities.

4. Active, active, active

The key to any possible success in your cramming will be the extent to which you are active in your first pass through the material you haven't seen before. You must also be active in the review and rehearsal. Output, output, output — this must be your mantra. Make sure that you are able to recall all of what you put in.

c. Sample 5-day plan

The essential idea underlying effective cramming is to use all the principles of regular exam preparation with only two variations. The first variation is obvious: you must compress all the steps into a much shorter time frame. The second variation is that you will likely have to allow time for learning some material for the first time.

Day 1

(a) 50% of your time

Read section **a.2.** of chapter 13 that deals with the steps of good exam preparation in the homestretch. Do all the preliminary activities (Steps 1 to 4).

Gather all material.

Make a schedule.

Do a two-hour review of all material (longer than a regular initial, but you will have to spend extra time on information you haven't covered before).

Create a menu of what you will concentrate on.

You will feel a great deal of pressure to get down to "real" studying instead of this preparatory stuff, but don't skip it. This is the stage that will help you identify the limited amount of material that will be your focus. If you don't focus your energy and merely skim over all the material, you are setting yourself up for failure.

You must make decisions about what to include on your menu. Remember, you only have 5 days to work. Use as many cues as possible to help you make your decisions: What did the instructor think was important? Are some topics too difficult for you? What subjects are clearly fundamental to the course?

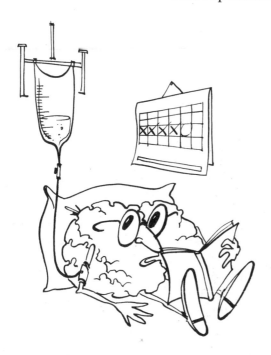

Set priorities for both the review of material and the first learning of new topics. Write them down.

(b) 25% of your time

Learn at least one of the topics that you are studying for the first time. No matter how much time you have available, don't study more than two new topics on one day. Start with the most important subjects.

(c) 25% of your time

Do an intensive review of the most important topics you have already learned at some level.

Day 2

(a)   25% of your time

Learn at least one of the topics that you are doing for the first time. No matter how much time you have available, don't study more than two new topics on one day.

(b) 25% of your time

Do an intensive review of the most important topics you have already learned at some level. Begin review of new material you learned on Day 1.

(c) 50% of your time

Do some output activities. This will be the most important part of your cramming. Make speeches; teach an understanding friend; answer practice questions; make mnemonic devices; create mind maps; write, write, write, write.

Day 3

(a) 15% of your time

Learn at least one of the topics that you are studying for the first time. No matter how much time you have available, don't study more than two new topics on one day.

(b) 35% of your time

Do an intensive review of the most important topics you have already learned at some level. Begin review of new material you learned on Day 2.

(c) 50% of your time

Work on output activities. This will be the most important part of your cramming. Make speeches; teach an understanding friend; answer practice questions; make mnemonic devices; create mind maps; write, write, write, write.

This takes a lot of energy, but keep it up. Get plenty of sleep.

Day 4 — the day before

(a) 10% of your time

Learn one more topic that you haven't covered before. If you have no more new subjects to cover, add this time to your review of new material you have learned in previous days.

(b) 10% of your time

Do an intensive review of the most important topics you have already learned at some level. Begin review of new material you learned on Day 3.

(c) 75% of your time

Do output activities. This will be the most important part of your cramming. Make speeches; teach an understanding friend; answer practice questions; make mnemonic devices; create mind maps; write, write, write, write.

Keep your energy up! Take frequent breaks and don't forget to rest and eat well.

(d) 5% of your time

Read the section in chapter 13 dealing with exam taking strategies. Anticipate what is coming, and devise a strategy for the coming exam experience.

Day 5 — the day of the exam

NO NEW MATERIAL. Do not try to learn anything new. You will probably feel tempted to try and cover just one more topic in the hours before the exam. It will compromise all the work you have done to this point if you give in to that temptation.

Review. Rehearse. Spend all your time going over what you already know, reviewing your exam strategy, and visualizing a positive result.

Bonus: Day 6 — the day after

Don't ever get yourself in that situation again. Start the 10-day program in chapter 17 to get started on the road to proper learning and study techniques. Raise the standards you expect of yourself. You have this amazing capacity for learning and study that can lead to spectacular academic achievement. Why waste it?

Challenge yourself to tap into that unused genius potential that exists inside everyone. Try two or three of the 10-day cycles and experience the improvement. What have you got to lose? You can always go back to your old habits later. If you enjoy the sensation of panic and failure that comes from last-minute cramming, it will still be there for you if you don't like the feeling of success. But it is more likely that the thrill of success will replace your addiction to mediocrity and just getting by.

That level of learning achievement is there for you if you really want it. Reach out and take it.

Index

A

accelerated learning 40, 52, 151

activated memory. *See* memory

active listening 130

active reading 120-123.
  See also study reading

active studying 60, 62, 69, 87-88, 104-105, 120-121, 135, 140, 150, 154, 191-194, 199; efficiency 137; flash cards 141; for cramming 207; for exams 157; listening 130; note making 122, writing 89. *See also* intelligences; learning modalities; study tools

Adams, Douglas 4

affirmations 42, 51-52, 178, 190; examples 51, 189; in exams 160. *See also* positive messages; self-esteem

Albinoni, Tommaso 54

alertness 112-113, 123, 125. *See also* relaxed alertness

alpha waves 24, 33, 53, 187

anticipation 121, 128, 130, 193; exams 158-159

Armstrong, Thomas 30

Astaire, Fred 87

attention span 75

audiotapes 136-137

auditory learning 26

axons 21

Ayer, A.J. 28

B

Bach, Johann Sebastian 54

Balfour, Lord 116

baroque music 53

Baruch, Bernard 85

Beethoven, Ludwig van 96

Bergson, Henri 141

beta waves 24

Bonaparte, Napoleon 117

Boucicault, Dion 107

brain 8, 17-30, 187; adaptability 4; and exercise 128; and memory 41, 59; and mind maps 150; and music 53; and oxygen 35, 40, 55; and sleep 140; and warm-up 112; as computer 10, 18, 87; background review 70; capacity 8, 11, 19, 21, 39; potential 9, 21, 83, 181, 199; research 17-19, 22-23, 27; two sides of 18, 22-23, 54, 187

brain density 21-22

brain waves 18, 23-25, 33, 73, 187; and music 52

breathing 40-41, 55, 190; exercises 43-45; in exams 166. *See also* relaxation

Bryan, William Jennings 98, 196

Buzan, Tony xiv, 71, 73, 144-145, 150-151, 181

C

calendars. *See* schedules; study tools

Carlyle, Thomas 141

Cervantes 145

Channing, William Ellery 121

Chesterfield, Lord 111

Chesterton, G.K. 38

children: and study program 9

Churchill, Winston 95, 139, 196

comfort zone 11, 13-14, 21, 39, 68, 87, 95, 124-125, 130, 179, 199

concentration 33-34, 38, 40, 75-82, 124-125; air quality 35, 76; distractions 76; fitness plan 80-81; improvement 77-82; length 70. *See also* distractions

Confucius 83

Corelli, Arcangelo 54

cortical brain 20-22; and relaxation 69; and stress 39, 166

If you have enjoyed this book and would like to receive a free catalogue of all Self-Counsel titles, please write to the appropriate address below:

Self-Counsel Press
1481 Charlotte Road
North Vancouver, BC
V7J 1H1

Self-Counsel Press
1704 N. State Street
Bellingham, WA
98225

Or visit us on the World Wide Web at *http://www.self-counsel.com*

Send the author your questions, comments, and suggestions about this book. Contact him at:

Kevin Paul
E-mail: kp@kevinpaul.com